TO LOVE THIS EARTHLY LIFE

TO LOVE THIS EARTHLY LIFE

❦

PATHWAYS THROUGH ECCLESIASTES

MICHAEL CASEY, OCSO

ORBIS BOOKS
Maryknoll, New York 10545

Founded in 1970, Orbis Books endeavors to publish works that enlighten the mind, nourish the spirit, and challenge the conscience. The publishing arm of the Maryknoll Fathers and Brothers, Orbis seeks to explore the global dimensions of the Christian faith and mission, to invite dialogue with diverse cultures and religious traditions, and to serve the cause of reconciliation and peace. The books published reflect the views of their authors and do not represent the official position of the Maryknoll Society. To learn more about Orbis Books, please visit our website at www.orbisbooks.com.

Imprimi potest, Abbot Steele Hartmann, April 22, 2021

The Scripture quotations from 1 Kings on pages 7 and 8 and from Proverbs on page 46 are from the New Revised Standard Version Bible: Catholic Edition, copyright © 1989, 1993, National Council of the Churches of Christ in the United States of America. Used by permission. All rights reserved worldwide.

Manufactured in the United States of America

Library of Congress Cataloging-in-Publication Data

Names: Casey, Michael, 1942- author.
Title: To love this earthly life : pathways through Ecclesiastes / Michael Casey, OCSO.
Description: Maryknoll, New York : Orbis Books, [2021] | Includes bibliographical references. | Summary: "A series of honest but upbeat reflections on themes in Ecclesiastes designed to make spiritual reading of the book more fruitful"— Provided by publisher.
Identifiers: LCCN 2021035156 (print) | LCCN 2021035157 (ebook) | ISBN 9781626984561 (print) | ISBN 9781608339198 (ebook)
Subjects: LCSH: Bible. Ecclesiastes—Theology.
Classification: LCC BS1475.52 .C37 2021 (print) | LCC BS1475.52 (ebook) | DDC 223/.806—dc23
LC record available at https://lccn.loc.gov/2021035156
LC ebook record available at https://lccn.loc.gov/2021035157

CONTENTS

INTRODUCTION

Emerson's famous dictum, "To be great is to be misunderstood," may well be applied to the author of the biblical Book of Ecclesiastes. The fact that many commentators are left puzzled after reading the book is, perhaps, an indication that it is well worth exploring its contents. Someone who has been described as agnostic, atheist, conformist, conservative, determinist, epicurean, existentialist, fatalist, iconoclastic, nihilist, pessimist, radical, realist, skeptic, and stoic, sounds like an interesting person.[1] Of course, each of these labels could be examined, documented, and subjected to scrutiny, but it is probably better to admit there is something of the truth in all of them and, then, to set ourselves the task of pondering how it is that they can cheerfully coexist.

King Solomon's wisdom was apparently recorded in a book (cf. 1 Kgs 11:41). And so Qoheleth assigns to this wise ruler the role of being the putative author of this book that he is writing centuries later, although this pretense is not maintained beyond the second chapter. Probably this presumed authorship was a factor in the book's acceptance as canonical by a

---

1. See W. Vogels, "Performance vaine et performance saine chez Qoheleth," *Nouvelle Revue Théologique* 113 (1991): 363–69.

meeting of rabbis at Jamnia (Jabneh) in 90 AD.[2] The ancient Christian tradition seems also to have taken the ascription at its face value. About the year 240, Origen composed his *Commentary on the Song of Songs* and mentions in his prologue that Solomon was the author of three biblical books: Proverbs, Ecclesiastes, and the Song of Songs.[3] Progressively, since the Enlightenment, it has become clear that Solomon was not the author of the book; it belongs to a later period in Israel's history. Far from being part of institutional Israel, the work of a king or a priest or a recognized prophet, the book's author is a quintessential outsider.

Because of the variety of viewpoints expressed in the book, some scholars have postulated a plural authorship. Others, like Pope Gregory the Great, think that the author employed the device of *prosopopoeia*, populating his text with different speakers, each expounding a different approach to the question.[4] Neither of these solutions is necessary.[5] The main part of the book is the work of a single author, although the epilogue is probably a redactional addition, possibly included with the intention of making it seem more conven-

---

2. The different arguments *pro* and *contra* are rehearsed in *Yadaim* 3.5. See *The Mishnah*, trans. Herbert Danby (Oxford: Oxford University Press, 1972), 781–82.

3. Origen, *The Song of Songs: Commentary and Homilies*, trans. R. P. Lawson, Ancient Christian Writers 26 (Westminster, MD: The Newman Press, 1957), 41.

4. Gregory the Great, *Dialogues* 4.4; *Sources Chrétiennes* 265, 26–32.

5. "There is, to be precise, an inner unity which can find expression otherwise than through a linear development of thought or through a logical progression in the thought process, namely through the unity of style and topic and theme, a unity which can make a work of literature into a whole and which can, in fact, give it the rank of a self-contained work of art." Gerhard von Rad, *Wisdom in Israel* (London: SCM Press, 1972), 227.

tional and, thereby, more acceptable for incorporation in an eventual canon.[6]

Following the example of other commentators, I will refer to the book by the term "Ecclesiastes," derived from the Greek; the author I will name as "Qoheleth," based on the Hebrew. The distinction is only a convenience. Both words refer to the *qahal* or assembly (*ecclesia*). By using this title, the author may be considered to be claiming to be a speaker, teacher, or preacher to the whole convocation of Israel. Qoheleth is not a name but a function which the author assigns to himself. He is one who gives a teaching to the people, written in the common idiom of his own day and addressed to his contemporaries.

The date most often assigned to Ecclesiastes by critical scholars is around 250 BC, that is, in the period of the Second Temple and during the Ptolemaic century. Little is known of what was happening in Palestine at this time. Apparently, it was a period of relative peace; tribute was paid to Egypt, and existing institutions functioned as previously. Under the Hellenistic Ptolemaic dynasty, the capital, Alexandria, was home to a significant Jewish diaspora, and would eventually produce a Greek translation of the Scriptures known as the Septuagint. Some of the issues with which Qoheleth was concerned he shared with Hellenistic thinkers, but there is no evidence to suggest direct linkage.

Experts tell us that the language of Ecclesiastes is typical of the period. It is a later form of Hebrew, with evidence of Aramaizing tendencies, sprinkled with words borrowed from Persian, and showing a familiarity with the vocabulary of all kinds of everyday realities, including the world of commerce. In a country located in the overlap of empires, a bastardized lingua

---

6. See Gerald T. Sheppard, "The Epilogue to Qoheleth as Theological Commentary," *Catholic Biblical Quarterly* 39, no. 2 (1977): 182–89.

franca is to be expected. It is not the idiom of the schools or of a religious elite. It is ordinary language with a secular tinge. Furthermore, many of the references that we would anticipate finding in a book of the Bible are absent. The divine Tetragrammaton (YHWH) is not used. Abraham, Isaac, and Jacob are not named, nor is Moses. The exodus is not referenced nor is the giving of the Law. The word *torah* is not found, although in the epilogue there is an admonition to keep the commandments (Eccl 12:13). Temple sacrifice is mentioned only dismissively (Eccl 5:1; 9:2). Rather than delivering a message from God, like the ancient prophets, Qoheleth describes what his own eyes have seen as the basis of further critical reflection. First-person use of the verb *r'h* "to see" is frequent (21 times) alongside the more general *yesh*, "there is" (15 times). What the book contains is not a series of esoteric abstractions but reflections on the commonplace experience of human life. It is the quality and depth of these reflections, not some certified membership of a specialized group, that mark the author as a sage (Eccl 12:9). The stance Qoheleth takes is similar to what Jeremiah had predicted, some three centuries earlier. The focus has moved away from traditional temple piety toward the autonomous use of human powers of observation and reasoning:

> It will come to pass that, when you have increased and become many in the land, in those days—an oracle of the Lord—they will no longer speak of the Ark of the Covenant of the Lord. It will not enter their hearts; they will not remember it. They will not seek it. And they will not make another one. (Jer 3:16)

This is to say that Qoheleth breathes an atmosphere different from what had prevailed in earlier centuries and the unsurprising result is a different kind of book.

From the time of the medieval Aristotelian Ibn Rushd (Averroës: 1126–1198), the task of interpretation has been considered to be a matter of translating symbolic discourse (for example, the Qur'an) into rational discourse. We would say moving it from right-brain categories into left-brain categories. This is the method that has been largely followed, especially in the West, and especially by those commentators who are more Aristotelian than Platonic, and closer to the school of Antioch than to that of Alexandria. Making sense of a poetic text by making it march to the tune of sequential logic enables it to deliver a clear message, but something is lost from the integrity of the text's meaning. In particular, the poetic appeal of a text may be diminished. Too much clarity may obscure the author's purpose in writing and, as a result, the authentic meaning may be missed.

A text that is puzzling needs to be approached from a different angle. Instead of beginning with the individual parts and trying to fit them together into a meaningful whole, perhaps it is wiser to begin with the whole. This is grasped intuitively on the basis of a comprehensive understanding of the complete text before undertaking a closer examination of the details. Of course, the whole that is perceived has constantly to be checked against the parts to ensure that the chance of rashly projecting meaning into the text is reduced.[7] First we accept the text as a whole, then we look at its parts. Every conclusion needs to be checked against the text in its totality. Otherwise bizarre explanations flourish. Roland Murphy exclaims, "How many far-fetched theories have been hazarded by modern writers who are locked up in their own crippling presuppositions?"[8]

---

7. See Hans-Georg Gadamer, *Truth and Method* (London: Sheed & Ward, 1975), 422: "The unfolding of the totality of meaning towards which understanding is directed, forces us to make conjectures and to take them back again. The self-cancellation of the interpretation makes it possible for the thing itself—the meaning of the text—to assert itself."

8. Roland Murphy, *Ecclesiastes* (Dallas: Word Books, 1992), lv–lvi. Among the dozen or so commentaries available to me, I have used

To many readers, the Book of Ecclesiastes appears like an unfinished jigsaw puzzle. Islands of meaning congeal, but the whole picture is not quickly apparent. In this case, incompletion is not an imperfection. This is the dominant message of the book. Qoheleth wishes to communicate that there is no clear-cut and complete answer to the mysteries of life. The apparent disarray is reflective of reality. The medium is the message. Only God knows the whole story. This is not the negation of meaning. It is simply the affirmation that a total grasp of cosmic meaning is beyond the limited range of human understanding—in the same way that quantum physics surpasses the intellectual capacity of even the brightest kindergarten child. Qoheleth aims to stimulate in us a peevish frustration that is an incentive to further reflection and, indeed, further exasperation. "From one angle or another, everything that is said is true."[9] It is the thinking and reflection that are important, not the arrival at some "final" conclusion.

Sapiential writings serve a purpose different from that pursued by the words of the prophets. Generally, the prophets address themselves to a particular situation and either denounce abuses or recommend a change of heart. They seek to influence the actions of their hearers. The purveyors of wisdom take a step back from immediate issues. Their words are directed at modifying attitudes, inviting the people to reflection rather than to decision and action. They are not so grounded in the historical situation, and they have a more universal message.

---

this one as a default point of reference. See also, from the same author, "On Translating Ecclesiastes," *Catholic Biblical Quarterly* 53, no. 4 (1991): 571–79, where the manifold difficulties involved in translating this book are noted and discussed.

9. W. Sibley Towner, "Ecclesiastes," in *The New Interpreter's Bible Commentary*, vol. 3 (Nashville, TN: Abingdon Press, 2015), 956.

Ecclesiastes has been described as "a notebook of ideas by a philosopher/theologian about the downside and upside of life."[10] The procedure followed by Qoheleth is not dissimilar from the approach embedded in Plato's *Symposium*. In that case, different speakers casually circle around the theme of love, without ever arriving at apodictic conclusions. To make sense of the whole discussion, the potential commentator must attempt "to indicate how these various themes are interwoven with apparent naturalness so as to shed light reciprocally upon one another."[11] Norbert Lohfink notes that "orderly logical concatenation is not the highest value in the kind of literature Qoheleth belongs to."[12] The purpose of the work is to stimulate readers to reflect for themselves on what is said—not necessarily to reach definitive answers, but to become more convinced that the questions are real and, therefore, worth pondering. Qoheleth seeks not to rob us of our doubts and difficulties, but instead to help us view them differently, so that we are able to live with them and not be dismayed. His viewpoint reflects the paradox that is glimpsed in the saying, "If anything is really true, then its opposite is also true."

In both form and content, Qoheleth shows himself to be something of an iconoclast. By this I do not mean that he had no respect for the sacred but, rather, that he was impatient with false claimants to sacredness. Those who easily attribute absolute value to what is not holy are demeaning true holiness. When an icon cannot bear the weight of the holiness attributed to it, whether it be a material representation or an institutional practice, it needs to be broken. This is an act of religion; it is not

---

10. Towner, "Ecclesiastes," 957.

11. W. Hamilton, introduction to *The Symposium*, by Plato (Harmondsworth: Penguin, 1959), 9.

12. Norbert Lohfink, "Qoheleth 5:17–19—Revelation by Joy," *Catholic Biblical Quarterly* 32, no. 4 (1990): 632.

anti-religious. According to C. S. Lewis, it is God who is the great iconoclast:

> Images of the Holy easily become holy images—sacrosanct. My idea of God is not a divine idea. It has to be shattered time after time. He shatters it himself. He is the great iconoclast. Could we not say that this shattering is one of the marks of His presence?...And most are offended by the iconoclasm, and blessed are those who are not.[13]

Understood in this context, Ecclesiastes is a supremely religious book. It refuses to attribute the qualities of God to any created reality, but insists on the contingency and precariousness of everything we encounter in the world around us. Furthermore, although Qoheleth's message has a unique and distinctive flavor, it is not unrelated to other parts of the Old Testament. For example, in the critical apparatus of the *New International Version* there are fifty-one marginal references to the Book of Proverbs and forty-one to the Book of Psalms, citing some thirty different psalms. It would seem that Ecclesiastes is not as much of an outlier as is sometimes assumed.

It is because of his characteristic propensity for deconstruction that Qoheleth has the capacity to speak powerfully to our generation. The Western Church in particular has been in the habit of wanting to maximize its dogmas and, thence, to analyze and define them in great detail. Parallel to this dogmatic expansion has been an ever-increasing and ever more detailed body of moral imperatives.[14] As we might have ex-

---

13. C. S. Lewis, *A Grief Observed* (London: Faber, 1987), 55–56.

14. The confusion of ethics and morality is widespread. Traditional moral theology recognizes a distinction between the objective science of *ethics* and the subjective contribution to an action, meas-

pected, inherent credibility faded when teachings became distant from their origins, so that recourse to institutional coer-
cion was required to support them. This has not been a
strategy likely to win the hearts of those who have come of age
in a period of high secularization. Such people have been encouraged to practice the art of deconstruction and to be suspi-
cious of all power structures and systems of enforcement. It is
probably no coincidence that the stronger the insistence on
conformity, the weaker the sense of belonging has become. No
doubt the drift away from formal Church adherence has been
intensified by revelations of systemic misconduct in sections of
the ecclesiastical bureaucracy and among a few religious high-
fliers. The mass media has not failed to keep us well informed
on such matters. What is especially tragic about this decline in
active membership is that many of those who have stood apart
from the institutional body never abandoned all elements of
the faith they had previously received. They have become
homeless believers, wandering sheep that find themselves outside the purview of their shepherds.[15]

Perhaps what is needed, in the face of expansionist tendencies within theology, is a trimmed-down body of doctrine that

---

ured by *morality*. In evaluating the moral character of an action, the
intention of the actor must be taken into account. A person is not held
accountable for an action done unintentionally. Nor can the conscience always be presumed to have absorbed the full weight of external precepts so that every action is necessarily carried out in full
awareness of its ethical character. Despite the misuse of the notion of
"situation ethics," the fact remains that moral perspective is shaped
by socialization. Even after catechesis, a person's conscience may not
be as finely tuned as one would hope. Fulminating against acts that a
person conscientiously considers inoffensive simply leads to a loss of
credibility. A subtler and more nuanced approach is needed.

15. This phenomenon is not confined to religious attachment.
See Peter L. Berger, Brigitte Berger, and Hansfried Kellner, *The Homeless Mind* (Harmondsworth: Penguin, 1974).

does not intrude into areas beyond its own competence. More fundamentally, perhaps, there may be scope for a move toward a more apophatic approach similar to that favored by the Eastern churches. This is a mode of theological discourse that seeks to maintain an aura of mystery, recognizing the limits of human intelligence when it comes to matters concerning the divinity, and directing itself more to wondering contemplation than to academic dialectic. It is sometimes termed "negative theology," because it celebrates what we do not know about God. It emphasizes the transcendence and, hence, the comprehensive unknowability of God: God is eternal, beyond time and space; God is immutable, unchanging; God is uncaused; God is ungendered; God has no form or color. To look on the "face" of God is to die. We know much about God by faith, and perhaps, even by reason, but, at best, we see through a glass darkly. This darkness is a significant part of our data about God.

The task of untangling what we do know as a result of God's self-revelation from its historically conditioned explanations and expansions is a formidable challenge. We receive the revelation encased in a shell that was suitable to its time, but it does not always adapt itself to the onrush of centuries. Disputes arise as to whether what is handed down in one time and place is the same as what others have received and believed. In trying to attain an unambiguous clarity of language, there is a constant danger of straining out gnats while swallowing camels. Here, as elsewhere, it is often wiser to pay more attention to the tides than to the eddies.

If we are so inclined, we may choose to see the Book of Ecclesiastes as a global critique of religious and philosophical ideology. It is an invitation to be somewhat reserved in our acceptance of the amplified generalizations included in what others tell us about the meaning of life. It calls us to recognize the limits of our knowledge and to remain within those limits; to make the most of what is possible for us without expending energy on reaching for the stars in an effort to master them. For Qoheleth, seeking to understand everything would be regarded as *hubris*. Wisdom, for him, consists in staying within our own sphere of existence. Our task is to look around and observe what is happening, to reflect on its possible meanings, and to tailor our discourse and our behavior in accordance with what we have understood. He is confident that the good life is within everyone's reach, if only they pay attention. His approach is much more nuanced than that of mere empiricism, because he includes in his purview of reality the presence and action of God. It is because of this invisible influence on human affairs that they are not fully comprehensible to limited human powers of knowing. If God is at work in everything that happens, then the ultimate meaning of what takes place around us is beyond our powers to ascertain. If the world of space and time is said to be beset by "vanity," it is because *we* are unable to perceive more than its superficial characteristics.

If Ecclesiastes is a critique of ideology, it is also a critique of prejudice, which often exercises its influence below the threshold of consciousness. If our prejudices also are to be submitted to systematic doubt, then those cherished by Qoheleth himself should also be examined. Because he is not formulating laws or writing a philosophical treatise, Qoheleth, also referred to as the Preacher, speaks from personal experience and, in that process, inevitably reveals some of his own limitations and prejudices. It would not be in the spirit of Ecclesiastes to overlook these liabilities. They need to be faced. For example, there is one text in Ecclesiastes that is particularly problematic in today's climate of thought and feeling—not in its intended meaning but in its content and expression. It is amusing to watch commentators scurrying to find shelter rather than admit the obvious meaning of the text. We are referring to a passage that seems to betray a belief that women are morally inferior to men:

And I find more bitter than death the woman whose heart is as nets and snares, and her hands, as bands: he that is good before God, shall be delivered from her, but the sinner shall be taken by her. Behold, saith the Preacher, this have I found, seeking one by one to find the count: And yet my soul seeketh, but I find it not: I have found one man of a thousand: but a woman among them all have I not found. Only lo! this have I found, that God hath made man righteous: but they have sought many inventions. (Eccl 7:26–29)

Is Qoheleth guilty of misogynistic tendencies, or is he just giving unthinking expression to the conventional prejudices of his time and class?[16]

There are two parts to the passage. The first expresses distaste for the fiercely seductive woman—with all the blame attaching to her, as if the male did not consent to be ensnared and bound. Yet we know that, on the contrary, seduction is a process whereby a stream of semi-conscious signals is exchanged between the parties. To claim a unilateral victimhood is to unreasonably deny complicity. It takes two to tangle! Qoheleth clearly views things from the male perspective and, as a result, his assessment of the situation is defective. And if the text is taken as a generalized statement of fact, it is clearly unfair. The interesting point he makes is that the degree of involvement in the process is an indicator of moral status; sinful men (and women) will fall into the trap; good men (and women) will escape.

---

16. It is perhaps worth noting that, of 405 citations of Ecclesiastes in seventeen Cistercian writers of the twelfth and thirteenth centuries, there is only a single citation of Eccl 7:28, and that was quoted only to refute it by reference to Prov 31:10–31, the story of the *mulier fortis*. See M. Casey, "Bernard and Ecclesiastes," *Cistercian Studies Quarterly* 56, no. 2 (2021): 191–209.

The second part carries the discussion further. How many will remain innocent? One man in a thousand is his estimate. This grandiose statement is not based on statistical evidence. It is almost a joke. But then he continues by saying that even fewer women are so virtuous. It does not matter whether we are affronted or amused by this gratuitous assertion. It seems to me that Qoheleth would be the last one to insist that we agree to everything he says. As a rule, he does not present us with conclusions to accept but with elements of an argument so that we can begin to resolve the matter for ourselves. We are not compelled to accept his male chauvinistic prejudices any more than we have to believe, as he did, that the world is flat. The point that he is making is that few—be they men or women—are entirely guiltless.

He continues by affirming that this is not how it was meant to be. God made humankind (the word used is gender-inclusive) to be upright, but the simple life is not for most of us. It seems that we prefer to complicate things with our many schemes and dreams and, generally, to go our own way and attempt to fashion our own future. That is a thought well worth pondering. Too often we ignore objective data on the basis of subjective preferences. In addition, many of the troubles we experience derive from some form of inner conflict which complicates the choices we make and eventually leads to undesirable outcomes. If we were to sort out some of our inner conflicts and cleanse our vision, a lot of our external troubles would disappear.

It is worth noting that the ideal of gender equality probably has its origins in the teaching of Saint Paul, though in most subsequent centuries the relevance of his insight has been watered down to the point of disappearance. In our generation, we are acutely aware of the issues gender equality raises, and this tends to shape our response to ancient texts. The fact that Qoheleth's attitudes reflect the time and culture in which he lived should not surprise us, but it is important that this deficiency should not serve as a pretext for ignoring the abundant wisdom that this book embodies.

————————

The title I have given this book, *To Love This Earthly Life*, may come as a surprise to some readers. Those who have only a slight acquaintance with Qoheleth sometimes regard him as a gloomy fellow. However, despite his robust iconoclasm, he is not a world-denier. His central point is, quite simply: Make the most of your life as it is, because it is the only one you will ever have; don't waste your energies on what does not matter. This means being mindful of the present moment and its potential. It will certainly not be all good. Every human situation is a variable combination of good and bad elements, not always in equal proportions. This is a matter of experience. Our attitude to life will depend on our choice of focus. If we allow ourselves to be invaded and dominated by negativity, our lives will be miserable and, probably, unproductive. We are best served by accepting our life as it is, and exerting every effort to make the most of it. This is reality. Living apart from reality is the road to madness. If we cannot love the reality we see, any love we profess toward what is unseen must be considered delusional. Our life is all that we have; it is not a rehearsal. So, let's get on with it.

As with a former book, I am using the Geneva Bible of 1562 as the default translation of Ecclesiastes; I have updated the spelling and occasionally made corrections to conform it more fully to the Hebrew original. My reasons for using this version are two. First, I wanted to distinguish the direct quotations of Ecclesiastes from my own words. Second, I hope that the slightly archaic language will invite readers to slow down, remembering that what they are reading comes from a distant culture and is over two thousand years old. Unfamiliarity has the effect of making us pay closer attention and serves us as a reminder of the inherent foreignness of the text we are reading. We have to struggle to come to terms with it. Ecclesiastes was never intended as a rapid answer to questions; if we can take more time to ponder its implications so much the better. For some readers it may be productive to compare the Geneva text with a more contemporary version, perhaps wondering at the way similar meanings are conveyed by different words. The important thing is to spend time with the text, allowing it to circulate through our daily experiences until questions similar to those that Qoheleth poses begin to surface in our minds and cause us to direct our thoughts to finding some answers.

In the process of writing this book I have spent quite a lot of time in its company, reading the text in different versions, checking out commentaries and trying to go deeper into some of its mysteries. I have found this to be a helpful and stimulating study, one revealing as much about myself as about Ecclesiastes. My conclusion is that pondering the wisdom of Qoheleth will be most useful for persons of a mellower age, that is, people who have had a fair amount of life experience and have reached the point where they will appreciate thinking more deeply about it. Inevitably, there will be many moments in the experience of a lifetime that seemed significant at the time and that no longer have much urgency or importance—we recognize them as "vanity." Their withdrawal into the background allows other elements of our history to assume a greater prominence. If we take Ecclesiastes seriously, it will probably seem like an invitation to rewrite our autobiography.

I have described the various themes discussed in this book as "pathways" through Ecclesiastes. The image is taken from the kind of notice often found at the entrance to national parks. If you want to see the waterfall, take this route. If you are interested in scenic views, take this trail. If you want a quick exposure to some of the most attractive features, follow this path. Each trajectory winds its way through the total area in such a manner that it exposes the visitor to different and complementary aspects of the whole. Similarly, the topics or themes discussed here each follow a different path through the whole book and expose the reader to different components of Qoheleth's thought. No attempt is made at synthesis. We are invited to sit back and enjoy what the author has written, to listen to its echoes in our own experience and, perhaps, to be influenced by what he has written in formulating our own philosophy of life.

I suggest that this book be read slowly and gently in a mood of reflection. My approach has been somewhat circular, as is Ecclesiastes itself, approaching the same texts from different angles to bring out the multiple meanings that they sometimes contain. It will serve best if this book is read simultaneously with the text of Ecclesiastes and with the book of experience, testing everything that is written against one's personal experience. I am suggesting that readers interpret this book as being mostly about themselves—rather than as philosophical reflections on the outside world. It can become a mirror in which they will see themselves more clearly and, from that vision, derive a greater acceptance and love of this earthly life—in all its mixity[17]—as somehow coming from the beneficent hand of God, leading them ultimately into a more abundant life. .

---

17. Human life is composed of different elements; not all of them sit together comfortably and some seem mutually hostile, but all of them belong to life's integrity.

1

VANITY

The opening blast of the Book of Ecclesiastes is one of the best-known verses of the Bible, though its precise meaning is not immediately clear.

> Vanity of vanities, saith the Preacher: vanity of vanities, all is vanity. (Eccl 1:1–2)

The "vanity of vanities" construction is the equivalent of a superlative, so the phrase means "ultimate vanity." But what is "vanity"? The most frequent sense in contemporary English is some form of narcissistic conceit or empty pride, but here an older meaning is suggested, a meaning not much different from the Latin *vanitas*. Saint Augustine understood vanity to be the diametric opposite to truth. Whereas truth is dense with inexhaustible meaning, vanity is hollow, empty and without substance.[1] Accordingly, the term "vanity" refers to whatever is futile, worthless, valueless, useless, unprofitable, devoid of real value, foolish, fruitless, empty, and unavailing. To apply the word without qualification to

---

1. Saint Augustine, *In Psalmum CXVIII Enarratio* 12.1, 17.5; *Corpus Christianorum* 140, 1700, see also 1721.

everything that exists is clearly an exaggeration, but what does Qoheleth really intend?

The word "vanity" is the translation of the Hebrew *hevel*. It is Qoheleth's signature term, occurring thirty-eight times in this book out of a total of seventy-three occurrences in the Hebrew Bible. The basic meaning is vapor or breath. The first characteristic of vapor is that it is insubstantial; it weighs virtually nothing. "The sons of Adam are *hevel*, the sons of men are but a lie; placed on a balance they rise; together they are *hevel*" (Ps 62:9).

A second feature is that it is temporary; vapor is impermanent. When a liquid evaporates, it becomes as nothing. Implied in both of these qualities is that *hevel* is worthless; there is no profit (*yitron*, a favorite word of Qoheleth) in pursuing it. Most often, the term is used as a metaphor, as a means of assigning a negative value to something, as we would describe a person as a "lightweight," meaning not to be taken seriously, even though, in fact, that person may be overweight.

> I have considered all the works that are done under the sun, and behold, all is vanity, and vexation of the spirit. (Eccl 1:14)

The meaning of the final phrase, *re'ut ruach* (here translated as "vexation of the spirit"), has been disputed for centuries. Around the end of the fourth century, Saint Jerome noted the different options;[2] these were still being rehearsed during the seventeenth century by Cornelius à Lapide.[3] The word *re'ut* appears seven times in Ecclesiastes (1:14; 2:11, 17,

2. Saint Jerome, *Commentarius in Ecclesiasten ad Paulam et Eustochium*, Preface; *Patrologia Latina* 23, 1061–1062.

3. Cornelius à Lapide, *Commentarii in Scripturam Sacram, Tomus IV* (Lyon: Pélagaud, 1854), 39–40.

26; 4:4, 6; 6:9) and its cousin *ra'yon* three times (1:17; 2:22; 4:16). The meaning of the two words has long been disputed. They are not found elsewhere. The Geneva Bible follows the Vulgate in attributing a subjective note to the phrase, translating it as "vexation of spirit." Associating with vanity upsets us and disturbs the equanimity of the human spirit.[4] In contrast, most modern commentators translate *ruach* as "wind" and prefer a translation that emphasizes vanity's objective futility. The Hebrew lexeme is mostly used in a shepherding context and can mean something like feeding or grazing. Following this, some would render the phrase as "feeding on the wind"—not the best basis for a healthy diet! Others more plausibly read the word as influenced by Aramaic and translate it as "chasing after the wind" or "striving after the wind." In other words, an exercise in futility. The various meanings are not incompatible; each conveys something of what Qoheleth is indicating.

Perhaps the best course is to keep all these various suggestions in mind whenever we encounter *hevel*. "Vanity" is a vapor with no clear form or function. It belongs to no category that the mind can create. It is beyond human power to attain and enjoy. It represents the *tohu wa-bohu* (formless void) that pre-existed creation—an aggressive resistance to any attempt to capture, contain, or control it. Vanity sows confusion in human hearts so that we do not really know what we know, and there is no constancy or consistency in striving after what we want. It is as though there were inherent in all things a force resistant to being that diminishes every expression of truth, goodness, and beauty. Its dirty fingers defile and deform everything it touches, and there is nothing on earth that

---

4. In the Vulgate Eccl 1:14, Saint Jerome translates the phrase as *afflictio spiritus*; in 6:19, he returns to *praesumptio spiritus*, which he used in his commentary and which was the rendering used in the Old Latin versions.

is exempt from its insidious invasions. Qoheleth seems to be implying that there is nothing in this world of space and time that possesses permanent and unqualified value. In a certain sense, there is nothing to which we need to assign an absolute value. Everything is in a state of constant flux. Nothing is a permanent and unqualified benefit. Mixity is the chief characteristic of the world of experience. Pure being does not belong to this earthly sphere. Unmixed truth, unmixed goodness, or unmixed beauty cannot be found here.

If *hevel* is an all-embracing component of human existence, then its meaning must be broad and not easily evoked in a single word. Hugh of Saint Victor (1096–1141) conjures up three overlapping senses that he understood in the word *vanitas* as applied to human existence: changeableness, its capacity for disproportionate attachment, and mortality:

> There are three kinds of *vanitas* of which this book [of Ecclesiastes] specifically treats. All vanity is included in them and [the author] asserts that everything under the sun is subject to them. The first is the vanity of changeableness which is in all transitory things by their nature. The second is the vanity of curiosity or cupidity which is in the minds of humans through their inordinate love for vain and passing things. The third is the vanity of mortality which belongs to human bodies by way of penalty.[5]

At this point, it may be useful to reflect on the nature of *hevel* according to the different aspects that it manifests. It can help sometimes if we go beyond the dictionary meaning of words and allow them to resonate at the emotional level. If I

---

5. Hugh of Saint Victor, *In Salomonis Ecclesiasten Homiliae XIX*, 1; *Patrologia Latina* 175, 118–119.

scan my personal library of experiences, I may find terms like crestfallen, disappointed, discontented, disgruntled, disillusioned, dissatisfied, frustrated, let down, and many more. These are all part of universal human experience that we may not repress. We need to recognize that these feelings are inevitable during our lifelong interaction with the real world. They are not necessarily aberrant. Taken collectively, these words tell me something about the impact that the objective "vanity" of everything has on my subjective disposition. On different days, different aspects may impact me more strongly but, if Qoheleth is to be believed, there will always be a profound dissonance between what I expect from life and what life actually delivers. As we shall see later, this is not always a disadvantage. A contrarian way of viewing this situation would be to say that reality always exceeds my expectations. These projections fall short of full reality; reality itself is not defective. This is an important qualification to bring to our reading of Ecclesiastes. There are things that are more important than the ones about which we care and make so much fuss.

Unsatisfying

Qoheleth begins his advocacy with a first-person case study, based on the character he initially appropriated and is about to discard: King Solomon. "Solomon" begins by describing his accumulation of wealth and his successful life. But there is a sting in the tail:

> I sought in mine heart to give myself to wine, and to lead mine heart in wisdom, and to take hold of folly, till I might see where is that goodness of the children of men, which they enjoy under the sun: the whole number of the days of their life. I have made my great

works: I have built me houses: I have planted me vine-yards. I have made me gardens and orchards, and planted in them trees of all fruit. I have made me cisterns of water, to water therewith the woods that grow with trees.

I have gotten servants and maids, and had children born in the house: also I had great possession of cattle and sheep above all that were before me in Jerusalem. I have gathered unto me also silver and gold, and the chief treasures of Kings and provinces: I have provided me men singers and women singers, and the delights of the sons of men, [and many women]. And I was great, and increased above all that were before me in Jerusalem: also my wisdom remained with me.

And whatsoever mine eyes desired, I withheld it not from them: I withdrew not mine heart from any joy: for mine heart rejoiced in all my labor: and this was my portion of all my travail. Then I looked on all my works that mine hands had wrought, and on the travail that I had labored to do: and behold, all is vanity and vexation of the spirit: and there is no profit under the sun. (Eccl 2:3–11)

In this Geneva translation there are, in these nine verses, thirty-six uses of first-person pronouns. What the text is describing is the ultimate in narcissistic self-indulgence. The king is very pleased with himself and happy with the life that he leads and all the benefits he enjoys. The First Book of Kings gives some indication of what Solomon had accumulated:

The weight of gold that came to Solomon in one year was six hundred sixty-six talents of gold, besides that which came from the traders and from the business of the merchants and from all the kings of Arabia and the governors of the land.... For the king had a fleet of ships of Tarshish at sea with the fleet of Hiram. Once every three years the fleet of ships of Tarshish used to come bringing gold, silver, ivory, apes and peacocks. ...Solomon gathered together chariots and horsemen; he had fourteen hundred chariots and twelve thousand horses which he stationed in the chariot cities and with the king in Jerusalem. The king made silver as common in Jerusalem as stones.... Among his wives were seven hundred princesses and three hundred concubines. (1 Kgs 10:14–15, 22, 26–27; 11:3, NRSV-CE)[6]

Solomon is described as living a life that represents the ultimate joy of men's desiring. Ancient kings were restrained by no constitutional barriers; they even could kill at whim (1 Kgs 2:25, 46). "Where the word of the King is, there is power, and who shall say unto him, What doest thou?" (Eccl 8:4). Kings did as they pleased, with no care for poverty, chastity, or obedience. During the early years of Solomon's reign the land enjoyed relative peace. He himself had a high reputation as a ruler, businessman, and international statesman. Nor was this high standing undeserved. For he was also known for his wisdom:

God gave Solomon very great wisdom, discernment and breadth of understanding as vast as the sand on the seashore, so that Solomon's wisdom surpassed the

---

6. Solomon's base annual income is calculated at 666 talents of gold. This amounts to about 50,000 lbs. or 800,000 oz., with a present-day value of over 1 billion dollars. And this was only a beginning. Solomon's marriages were not so much romantic liaisons but were probably meant not only to increase his wealth but also to reinforce political alliances with neighboring powers, acting as a tactic to safeguard the borders of his territory.

wisdom of all the people of the east and all the wisdom of Egypt. (1 Kgs 4:29–30, NRSV-CE)

Behold, I am become great, and excel in wisdom all
them that have been before me in Jerusalem: and mine
heart hath seen much wisdom and knowledge. And I
gave mine heart to know wisdom and knowledge,
madness and foolishness. (Eccl 1:16–17)

Outward wealth was complemented by interior riches.
Nothing that is desirable was lacking to the king's life. But, as
if to demonstrate that riches and religion do not co-exist for
long, Solomon fell away from his service of God. Receiving
everything he desired was not enough for him. "His heart was
not true to the LORD, his God" (1 Kgs 11:4, NRSV-CE). Human
desire is insatiable; no amount of accumulation can quench its
yearnings for more. And along with that desire, the mysterious inclination to deviance from goodness and separation
from God remains active.

After this build-up, Qoheleth puts on the lips of Solomon
a judgment regarding the worth of such a life with all its toil
and all its achievements: "Then I looked on all my works that
mine hands had wrought, and on the travail that I had labored
to do: and behold, all is vanity and vexation of the spirit: and
there is no profit under the sun" (Eccl 2:11). As for wisdom, "I
knew also that this is a vexation of the spirit. For in the multitude of wisdom is much grief: and he that increaseth knowledge, increaseth sorrow" (Eccl 1:17–18). He admits that
wisdom is superior to foolishness, but it too is subject to *hevel*
and is not immune from the universal fate of death.

Then I saw that there is profit in wisdom, more than in
folly: as the light is more excellent than darkness. For
the wise man's eyes are in his head, but the fool
walketh in darkness: yet I know also that the same

condition falleth to them all. Then I thought in mine heart, it befalleth unto me, as it befalleth to the fool. Why therefore do I then labor to be more wise? And I said in mine heart, that this also is vanity.

For there shall be no remembrance of the wise, nor of the fool for ever: for [all] that now is, in the days to come shall all be forgotten. And how dieth the wise man, as doth the fool? Therefore I hated life: for the work that is wrought under the sun is grievous unto me: for all is vanity, and vexation of the spirit.

I hated also all my labor, wherein I had travailed under the sun, which I shall leave to the man that shall be after me. And who knoweth whether he shall be wise or foolish? Yet shall he have rule over all my labor, wherein I have travailed, and wherein I have shewed myself wise under the sun. This is also vanity. (Eccl 2:13–19)

It will be noted that "Solomon" uses the same methodology as Qoheleth does throughout his book: "I saw...I know...I thought...I said." Observation of the world around him, understanding it, pondering its meaning, are the preludes to speech.[7] The main generator of wisdom in Ecclesiastes is the human power to reflect on reality and derive from it practical conclusions about how to conduct one's life. As we have noted, there is much less explicit reliance on the formulations of the Law.

"Solomon" testifies that there is no value in acquiring all that one desires. Possessions, pleasures, freedom, a high reputation, and even wisdom itself cannot fill the emptiness of the human heart. In their absence, such things seem to be worth

---

7. According to Sherlock Holmes, observation, knowledge, and deduction are the marks of a good detective. Arthur Conan Doyle, "A Study in Scarlet," in *Sherlock Holmes: The Complete Illustrated Novels* (London: Chancellor Press, 1987), 11.

pursuing, but once they are obtained, they are found to be no more than a puff of wind. It is discovered that their attraction was illusory, almost like a mirage in the desert. Only in taking hold of them did their insubstantiality become obvious. "Vanity of vanities; all is vanity."

Yet this affirmation of universal vanity is not a denial of the intrinsic goodness of everything that has been created. It is simply a statement that even when there is a colossal abundance of such benefits, the human heart is unsatisfied—just as unsatisfied as if it had nothing. The difference that possession of such desired benefits confers is minimal:

> Better is a handful with quietness, than two handfuls with labor and vexation of spirit. (Eccl 4:6)

> He that loveth silver, shall not be satisfied with silver, and he that loveth riches, shall be without the fruit thereof: this also is vanity. When goods increase, they are increased that eat them: and what good cometh to the owners thereof, but the beholding thereof with their eyes? The sleep of him that travaileth, is sweet, whether he eat little or much: but the satiety of the rich will not suffer him to sleep. (Eccl 5:8–12)

> There is an evil, which I saw under the sun, and it is much among men: A man to whom God hath given riches and treasures and honor, and he wanteth nothing for his soul of all that it desireth: but God giveth him not power to eat thereof, but a strange man shall eat it up: this is vanity, and this is an evil sickness. (Eccl 6:2)

What has been observed and noticed and pondered is the fact that riches do not necessarily make people content. Surveys have shown that not all winners of lotteries become happier; for some, their lives are ruined. It seems, as the Irving

Berlin song lamented many years ago, "After you get what you want, you don't want it." Nothing in the visible world of space and time can bring us that all-inclusive sense of fulfillment that deep down we desire. There is a profound lesson here: most of us believe that our lives would be happier if only we had more of what Solomon had: power, riches, possessions, sexual opportunities, reputation. Qoheleth casts doubt on that presupposition. He points to the example of Solomon and concludes that even the most complete realization of such fantasies will not lead to any permanent improvement in our happiness. Everything thus desired is *hevel*. For real happiness we must look elsewhere.

And there is more. The prized possession of wisdom, valued though it is, does not automatically make a person happier. Sometimes mindlessness can seem a lighter burden to carry. To be unaware of danger is to live without dread even though disaster threatens. Awareness of an imminent threat does not necessarily contribute to its avoidance, but will certainly render us unhappier by anticipating what is about to happen. On balance, "Solomon" thinks there is not much to choose between wisdom and folly:

> For what hath the wise man more than the fool? (Eccl 6:8)

> And I gave mine heart to know wisdom and knowledge, madness and foolishness: I knew also that this is a vexation of the spirit. For in the multitude of wisdom is much grief: and he that increaseth knowledge, increaseth sorrow. (Eccl 1:17–18)

The wisdom that Qoheleth recommends is the wisdom that comes from a fuller awareness of its own limitations. As we shall see later in this book, knowledge involves bringing both past and future to bear on the present. As a result, any potential gladness the present moment may hold can be marred by memories of bad things in the past, and by the distraction of trying to deal with what does not yet have any reality. The wider our consciousness of past and future, the less likelihood that we will rejoice unabashedly in present good fortune.

The ultimate vanquisher of all delusions is death, to which all alike are subject. This is a theme to which Qoheleth will return several times. As with Heidegger's understanding that the human is a *Sein zum Tode* (a being-toward-death), so the Preacher argues that searching for the ultimate meaning of human reality must consider the universal prospect of death. Whatever we gain or seem to gain in our lifetime is brought to nothing by our inevitable descent into the grave:

> As he came forth of his mother's belly, he shall return naked to go as he came, and shall bear away nothing of his labor, which he hath caused to pass by his hand. (Eccl 5:15)

> Shall not all go to one place? (Eccl 6:6)

> I considered in mine heart the state of the children of men that God had purged them: yet to see too, they are in themselves as beasts. For the condition of the children of men, and the condition of beasts are even as one condition unto them. As the one dieth, so dieth the other: for they have all one breath, and there is no excellency of man above the beast: for all is vanity. All go to one place, and all was of the dust, and all shall return to the dust. Who knoweth whether the spirit of man ascend upward, and the spirit of the beast descend downward to the earth? (Eccl 3:18–21)

Since we are all destined to die, it follows that our link with everything we seem to possess is impermanent. All material possessions have an inherent expiry date. Ownership ceases when life ends. It does not matter whether we have much or little: we cannot take what we have into the grave. What we claim to own is only leased. If our happiness is entirely dependent on possessions, then it will be lost when these are taken from us.

The profound empiricism of the author does not allow him to affirm what he cannot see. And what he sees is that at the end of their lives human beings descend into the grave, exactly as animals do, and no more is heard of them. For the rest, "Who knoweth?" This is not necessarily the denial of an afterlife; it is simply the common-sense conclusion that all we can see is death. Beyond that we know nothing.

The fact that all the things that we see around us lack the capacity to bring us ultimate satisfaction means that it is foolish for us to seek perfect fulfillment through their agency. This is not to say that the things around us are of little worth. It is, rather, to imply that our inherent desire is so large that it cannot be satisfied by whatever is limited to spatio-temporal existence. Such things are what they are. What is foolish, however, is to exaggerate their value and to pursue them with disproportionate vigor. The energies expended in this ultimately fruitless endeavor could have been utilized in more profitable employment. Seeking such worthless objects is not only a waste of personal resources, it also leads to a distortion in a person's scale of values and, thence, to a distorted view of reality. As Saint Bernard of Clairvaux notes, "The appetite for vanity is contempt of the truth; and contempt of the truth is the cause of our blindness."[8] It is not things that are foolish; we are foolish—to the extent that we allow ourselves to be seduced by them.

---

8. Bernard of Clairvaux, Letter 18.1; *Sancti Bernardi Opera* (Rome: Editiones Cistercienses, 1957–1978), 7:67. For more detail see M. Casey, "Bernard and Ecclesiastes," *Cistercian Studies Quarterly* 56, no. 2 (2021): 191–209.

Wasting time on such trivialities is "a foolish labor, affliction of spirit, the disemboweling (*evisceratio*) of the mind, and the emptying out of grace."[9] We can never be satisfied by them.

Insubstantial

The Hebrew word for God's glory is *kabod*. Its meaning derives from the notion of weight or heaviness. It signifies the acute density of divine being. By contrast, everything we experience in the world of space and time lacks this density; it is light-weight, insubstantial. Everything to which we attribute much importance does not have the capacity to bear the significance that we attribute to it. This is how Saint Gregory of Nyssa (335–395) reflects on this aspect of vanity:

> This is human life: a grain of sand (*psammos*) is the love of honor, a grain of sand power, a grain of sand riches, a grain of sand is everything we enjoy with fleshly urgency. In these things which will not last, for their sake infantile souls vainly labor, enduring many evils.[10]

According to Gregory, nothing in the realm of the flesh—that is, nothing in this world of space and time—is capable of truly enriching us. There are merely surface advantages desirable only to those whose desire goes no deeper. That is why material reality can never fully satisfy the questing human

---

9. Bernard of Clairvaux, *De Consideratione* 1.3; *Sancti Bernardi Opera* 3:396–97.

10. Gregory of Nyssa, *On Solomon's Ecclesiastes* 1; *Patrologia Graeca* 44, 628D; *Sources Chrétiennes* 416, 132. The image is probably drawn from Wisdom 7:9.

heart which is always seeking that which is beyond its reach, and even that of which it has not caught the merest sight.

> All the labor of man is for his mouth: yet the soul is not filled. For what hath the wise man more than the fool? What hath the poor that knoweth how to walk before the living? The sight of the eye is better than to walk in the lusts: this also is vanity, and vexation of spirit. (Eccl 6:7–9)

The mouth can be filled, and the belly also, but appetite is recurrent. Consumption is more likely to inflame desire so that it seeks more, rather than to extinguish it. "He that loveth silver, shall not be satisfied with silver, and he that loveth riches, shall be without the fruit thereof: this also is vanity" (Eccl 5:10). The energy expended on what has no value is wasted. "What profit hath he that he hath travailed for the wind?" (Eccl 5:15).

The image of *ruach*, as breath or wind, confirms this insubstantiality. To the unscientific eye, wind seems to be a force or movement without mass. Wind cannot be sensed except through the objects it affects. Of itself, it weighs nothing. In some of the Greek translations such as that of Symmachus, *hevel* is rendered by *atmos*, meaning breath or vapor—as close to nothing as one can imagine. Humans are inclined to invest their energies in what is insubstantial, because they, too, are close to nothing. The Psalmist is aware of this precariousness:

> O Lord, make me know my end, and the number of my days. Let me know how fleeting is my life. Behold, you have given me a small measure of days; the span of my life is as nothing before you. *Hevel* is everyone who stands. Indeed, those who go about are like a fleeting image. Indeed, they are *hevel*, they rush around and

heap up riches and do not know who will acquire them....Indeed, all humans are *hevel*. (Ps 39:4–6, 11)

Impermanent

Another manifestation of the vanity of things and of human beings is that all alike are ephemeral. They last but a day. In contrast to the agelessness of God, their past is recent and their future uncertain, but certainly brief. Any investment in that future necessarily must be conditional. Human life is short and we flit through our days like a shadow (Eccl 6:12). Qoheleth admonishes us that there is a season for everything (Eccl 3:1–8); everything comes and goes. All visible reality is transient and thus uncontrollable and, thereby, unpredictable:

> For he knoweth not that which shall be: for who can tell him when it shall be? Man is not lord over the [wind] to [control the wind]: neither hath he power in the day of death. (Eccl 8:7–8)

Like other biblical authors, Qoheleth understands that the universal reality of death renders any human life less than absolute. No matter how powerful or wise a person may seem, the day of death will put an end to any claim to being special. Like wild vegetation, human beings have a short period in which to blossom and bear fruit, but their end is not far away:

> You return humans to dust and say, "Return, sons of Adam." In your eyes a thousand years pass by like yesterday, a watch in the night. You sweep them away in death, like new grass in the morning. In the morning, it sprouts and springs, by evening it withers and dies....Indeed, all our days pass away in your wrath.

We end our years with a sigh. Our days are seventy years or eighty for the strong. And most of these are labor and grief. They pass swiftly and we fly away. ... Teach us to number our days that we may gain wisdom of heart. (Ps 90:3–6, 9–10, 12)

It is only to the extent that we are mindful of our death that we may be persuaded to take seriously the opportunities of the present, "before the sun and the light and the moon and the stars grow dark" (Eccl 12:2). Even now, the process of death is at work in us:

My days vanish like smoke and I wither away like grass. (Ps 102:3)

Remember, Lord, that my life is fleeting, and for what futility you created all the sons of Adam. Who can live and not see death or save themselves from the hand of Sheol? (Ps 89:47–48)

Useless

One of Qoheleth's key measures of value is profitability; does a course of action yield a good result, a profit (*yitron*)? If something is unprofitable, then it is useless. "It is evident that the term *hevel* describes something that is without merit, an unreliable, probably useless thing."[11] See, for example:

What profit hath he that worketh of the thing wherein he hath travaileth?" (Eccl 3:9)

---

11. Sibley Towner, "Ecclesiastes," in *The New Interpreter's Bible Commentary* (Nashville, TN: Abingdon Press, 2015), 3:958.

And what profit hath he that he hath travaileth for the wind? (Eccl 5:16)

Then I looked on all my works that mine hands had wrought, and on the travail that I had labored to do: and behold, all is vanity and vexation of the spirit: and there is no profit under the sun. (Eccl 2:11)

Qoheleth frequently contrasts the effort and grief involved in toil with the minimal benefits such labor confers. We work hard but gain little. If toil is fruitless, then it must owe its origin to some insatiable inner compulsion.[12] If there is disproportion between cause and effect, between promise and fulfillment, then disappointment and frustration will necessarily follow. "The mountains may have been in childbirth but all that is born is a ridiculous mouse."[13] Qoheleth is making the point that hard work is no guarantee of a good result. Even wisdom does not necessarily yield tangible benefits. "Why therefore do I then labor to be more wise? And I said in mine heart, that this also is vanity" (Eccl 2:15). "For what hath the wise man more than the fool?" (Eccl 6:8).

All human effort, therefore, is subject to the law of vanity. There is some inherent blockage in all our activities that often obstructs or prevents the linkage of cause and effect. Wisdom literature usually heaps much praise on the diligent worker, but Qoheleth understands that, praiseworthy as such diligence is, there is no guarantee that it will reap the rewards for which it had hoped.

---

12. A story told in Saint John Cassian's ninth conference illustrates this dynamic; a monk labors beyond reasonable limits because he is urged to do so by an unseen demon. The text can be found below in chapter 5.

13. Horace, *Ars poetica* I.139: *parturient montes, nascetur ridiculus mus.*

I returned, and I saw under the sun that the race is not
to the swift, nor the battle to the strong, nor yet bread
to the wise, nor also riches to men of understanding,
neither yet favor to men of knowledge: but time and
chance cometh to them all. For neither doth man know
his time, but as the fishes which are taken in an evil
net, and as the birds that are caught in the snare: so are
the children of men snared in the evil time when it falleth upon them suddenly. (Eccl 9:11–12)

We live in a world that seems to be subject to chance because we are unable to comprehend the invisible factors affect-
ing the outcome of all that we do.

Unreliable

Though the natural world runs according to determinable
rhythms (cf. Eccl 1:5–7), the same cannot be said about the society which humans have created for themselves. The smooth
flow of causality is often interrupted by discordant human in-
tervention. Qoheleth cites a particular example of unfairness: a
poor man saves his city but receives no credit for this:

I have also seen this wisdom under the sun, and it is
great unto me. A little city and few men in it, and a great
King came against it, and compassed it about, and built
forts against it. And there was found therein a poor and
wise man, and he delivered the city by his wisdom: but
none remembered this poor man. Then said I, Better is
wisdom than strength: yet the wisdom of the poor is de-
spised, and his words are not heard. (Eccl 9:13–16)

From a particular instance, Qoheleth derives a general
principle: goodness and wisdom are not always rewarded in

this life and foolish wickedness often escapes retribution. In this he is repeating the earlier prophetic lament, "Why does the way of the wicked prosper?" (Jer 12:1). Moreover, rank is no guarantee of quality. The Preacher observes that fools often occupy positions of honor and power (cf. Eccl 10:6) and unworthy kings surround themselves with equally unworthy courtiers (cf. Eccl 10:16):

> I have seen all things in the days of my vanity: there is a just man that perisheth in his justice, and there is a wicked man that continueth long in his malice. (Eccl 7:15)

> There is a vanity, which is done upon the earth, that there be righteous men to whom it cometh according to the work of the wicked: and there be wicked men to whom it cometh according to the work of the just: I thought also that this is vanity. (Eccl 8:14)

Even our grip on honestly earned material goods is tenuous. We cannot be sure that those to whom we bequeath our earthly goods will be worthy recipients. They are likely to undervalue what they receive if it comes to them without any effort. Moreover, the things we cherish will scarcely survive us, and all that we have invested in their acquisition will be totally lost:

> Therefore I hated life: for the work that is wrought under the sun is grievous unto me: for all is vanity, and vexation of the spirit. I hated also all my labor, wherein I had travailed under the sun, which I shall leave to the man that shall be after me. And who knoweth whether he shall be wise or foolish? Yet shall he have rule over all my labor, wherein I have travailed, and wherein I

have shewed myself wise under the sun. This is also vanity. Therefore I went about to make mine heart abhor all the labor wherein I had travailed under the sun. For there is a man whose travail is in wisdom, and in knowledge and in equity: yet to a man that hath not travailed herein, shall he give his portion: this also is vanity and a great grief. For what hath man of all his travail and grief of his heart, wherein he hath travailed under the sun? For all his days are sorrows, and his travail grief: his heart also taketh not rest in the night: which also is vanity. (Eccl 2:18–23)

No student of social history will ever argue that society evolves in a completely rational manner, totally unaffected by adventitious events and the actions of those outside its borders. Nor can it be doubted that "absolute power corrupts absolutely," whether this power is invested in an individual, in a group, or in the whole population. Even when philosophers become kings, tyranny is often the result. The elite enjoy privileges while the majority are oppressed. Satisfied with "bread and circuses," the populace cannot begin to comprehend the forces by which their lives are shaped. If, perchance, there are wise persons living among them, they are completely baffled by the relentless irrationality that engulfs them. Little that happens in that society today makes any sense, so that what will happen tomorrow nobody can dare to predict with any assurance of certainty.

Absurd

It has been suggested that the term "absurd," used by existentialist philosophers such as Søren Kierkegaard and Albert Camus, might be a fitting translation for *hevel*. In such a scenario, there is no God, the universe lacks any inherent meaning, and so, the translation of *hevel* as "meaningless" becomes plausible. Individuals may construct their own meaning by embracing the absurd and making the most of it. This is a task done necessarily in isolation and may be seen as anti-social, revolutionary, or even anarchist. Furthermore, it is an outlook that has no claim to continuing relevance, since it will necessarily cease when the individual dies. It is an attitude not far removed from nihilism. Rabbi Rami Shapiro is reluctant to admit the blanket use of this term in the case of Ecclesiastes:

> Absurdity is such only when played out against a background of fixedness and surety. It is only when we insist that life should be good, fair, just, and the like, can we speak of life being absurd for not living up to our ideas and ideals.[14]

What is seen as absurd and meaningless in a particular instance is so only because of the unacknowledged expectation that things would and should have been different. The position of Qoheleth is much more nuanced. It involves reflecting on the interchange of opposites to extract from it some measure of wisdom, and intelligently exploiting the variability of everything to extract from it such enjoyment as is possible, so that life becomes not merely tolerable but positively pleasurable.[15]

What distinguishes Qoheleth from the existentialists is his underlying acceptance that God exists. This will be explored in the next chapter. The Preacher's theism colors his understand-

---

14. Rami Shapiro, *Ecclesiastes Annotated and Explained* (Woodstock, VT: SkyLight Paths, 2010), xxx.

15. "An absurdity is not necessarily ephemeral ('a vapor'). It may in fact go on and on. But it makes no more sense at the end than it did at the beginning." Towner, "Ecclesiastes," 3:965.

ing of *hevel*. In some sense, what he is affirming is that compared with ultimate reality, everything else, the world of our everyday experience, is emptiness, impermanence, and insubstantiality. God is the absolute; everything else is contingent on God.

Contingent

Context is everything. Taken out of context, some passages in Ecclesiastes may easily seem like expressions of the direst pessimism. They are not. The book needs to be read as a whole, and its method of advancing an argument by apparent contradictions must be taken into account. The purpose of the book is not to arrive at a series of definitive conclusions, but to confront the reader with the refusal of the world of everyday experience to fit into the convenient categories of conventional human thought. The message is that we are unable to comprehend the universe, not that the universe itself is incomprehensible. The fact that we cannot make sense of reality does not necessarily mean that everything is senseless. Ecclesiastes is a book about the limitations of our intelligence. We become frustrated not because the world is frustrating, but because we lack the intellectual and emotional capacity to deal with the world as it is. We project onto the world our own limitations.

There is more. The book unabashedly belongs to the religious tradition of Israel. Even though, like the Book of Job, it seemingly subjects that tradition to a rigorous critique, it does not locate itself outside that tradition. Some would say that it is a good example of the Jewish love of verbal jousting and debate. Different perspectives are advanced with a view to stimulating reflection. There is a near-scrupulous avoidance of any facile simplification. And this trains us to have strong reservations about answers that are provided before the questions are asked. In some sense, the book may be viewed as an adaptation of the prophetic tradition, exposing the weakness of perfunctory religious belief and practice, and demanding something more rigorous.

The uncertainty that bedevils our history derives from the fact that the world in which we live is not autonomous. Events occur that are beyond our power to prevent or deflect. The most that we can do is to scurry around, after the fact, trying to minimize the damage or make the most of any opportunity. We are not in total control of what happens. Any arrangements that we make are always conditional. Tomorrow I shall begin another chapter of this book—if I do not die in my sleep tonight.

Is it possible that Qoheleth took his reflection a step further to ask whether human existence is precarious because it is not autonomous? To answer this in the affirmative is to suggest that the universe is dependent on something outside itself. In this case, the world of experience must be assayed in the context of a reality that may be described as transcendent or ultimate or absolute. If the world was created and is sustained by a reality outside itself, then it must be less than that from which it holds its existence. This was the manner by which many ancient theologians reconciled the perceived negativity of Ecclesiastes with their faith. Thus, Saint Jerome argues that the value of created things is relative: "In this way, we also can say that the sky and the earth and the sea and all that is contained in this circle, although they are good in themselves (*per se*), compared to God they may be said to be nothing."[16] And the *Glossa ordinaria*: "All is good that is created by the one who is good, but in its own order. Compared to God it must be reckoned as nothing, since it is transient and subject to decay."[17] To the extent that it was Qoheleth's intent to

---

16. Saint Jerome, *Commentarius in Ecclesiasten*; *Patrologia Latina* 23, 1066A.

17. Jennifer Lynn Kostoff Käärd, "The 'Glossa Ordinaria' on Ec-

demonstrate that all that is accessible to us through sense and intellect is of less significance than what transcends the limits of our perception, then our reading of his text needs to avoid overemphasizing its negativity. It may be like the case of the iceberg; there is much more to the total reality than what we can see. Qoheleth's writing seems negative only because it is pointing beyond the limited purview of our intelligence to something greater.

Friedrich Schleiermacher defined the religious sense as an experience or feeling (*Gefühl*) of absolute dependence.[18] This is to suggest that religion first manifests itself as an intuition or instinct that somehow our very being derives from elsewhere. If we feel somehow connected with an invisible or spiritual world, it makes sense that we would make some attempt to establish a linkage to our point of origin and, thence, to allow this connection to influence the choices that we make and the way that we act. If we are dependent on the spiritual world, the choices that we make should reflect the dependence that we feel. This, of course, is to go far beyond what Qoheleth is suggesting. He is making the point that nothing that we see around us can be considered as absolute. All is relative; relative to what is a question that is left hanging.

> Vanity of vanities, saith the Preacher: vanity of
> vanities, all is vanity. (Eccl 1:1–2)

The search for answers to the riddle of the universe is fruitful insofar as it allows us to discover that if such answers exist,

---

clesiastes: A Critical Edition with Introduction" (doctoral dissertation, University of Toronto, 2015), 182.

18. See Friedrich Schleiermacher, *On Religion: Speeches to Its Cultured Despisers*, trans. John Oman (Louisville, KY: Westminster/John Knox Press, 1994).

they are beyond our puny grasp. Ecclesiastes is a book about us, not about the universe. Meanwhile, its underlying message is that we should stop worrying about our limitations and get on with our lives. And enjoy them. Nothing else matters.

Perhaps, also, Qoheleth would have agreed with Chaucer's exhortation to youth that they turn from worldly vanity and turn instead to their Creator and source:

> O young fresh folks, he or she,
> in which that love up-groweth with your age,
> Repaireth home from worldly vanity,
> And of your heart up-casteth the visage
> To this God that after his image
> You made, and thinketh all is nothing but a fair,
> This world that passeth soon as flowers bloom.[19]

In other words, the advice seems to suggest that we recognize the ephemeral vanity of all that is around us and return to the source from which we come. It implies a move from what is partial toward a more expansive reality. This is probably the core message not only of all religions but also of many philosophies.

---

19. Geoffrey Chaucer, *Troilus and Cressida* V, §263 (slightly adapted).

2

GOD

To many readers, God seems absent from Ecclesiastes. They may be surprised to learn that the word *'elohim* occurs no fewer than thirty-seven times in the course of the book.[1] What is unusual is that twenty-nine of these have the definite article attached to the noun, *ha'elohim*, "the God." These references are often prolonged by the onward use of pronouns referring back to God. As we have already mentioned, the divine Tetragrammaton, YHWH, does not appear in Ecclesiastes. The sacred writer no longer speaks oracles from God but draws his message from human experience. And part of that message is a distinctive approach to questions concerning the divinity. His stance is more philosophical than historical. The God about whom Qoheleth speaks is also accessible to non-Jews. Rabbi Rami Shapiro asserts that, in this book, God is seen as "the absolute reality that shapes the relative world you and I experience every day."[2] This is to leave unsaid much of what

---

1. 1:13; <u>2:24</u>, <u>26</u>; 3:10, <u>11</u>, 13, <u>14</u>, <u>15</u>, <u>17</u>, <u>18</u>; <u>4:17</u>; <u>5:1</u>, 3, <u>5</u>, <u>6</u>, <u>17</u>, <u>18</u>, <u>19</u>; <u>6:2</u>; <u>7:13</u>, <u>14</u>, 18, <u>26</u>, <u>29</u>; 8:2, <u>12</u>, 13, <u>15</u>, <u>17</u>; <u>9:1</u>, <u>7</u>; <u>11:5</u>, <u>9</u>; <u>12:7</u>, <u>13</u>, <u>14</u>. The underlined references attach the definite article to the noun: *ha'elohim*.

2. Rami Shapiro, *Ecclesiastes Annotated and Explained* (Woodstock, VT: SkyLight Paths, 2010), xxxii.

the rest of the Bible affirms about God; not necessarily to deny it, but to turn attention to a different perspective.

It is important to remember that Israel's God always lacked definition but was described by means of the divine interventions in Israel's history: the call of Abraham and the promises made to him; the deliverance from Egypt; and the covenant concluded on Mount Sinai. Embarrassingly, Israel's God had a name that could not be spoken but voiced only as a riddle. The Septuagint translation tries to make sense of matters with the translation, "I am the One who is." This is an admirable invitation to metaphysical speculation, but it leaves the divine nature in the sphere of abstraction. The Canaanite deities El, Asherah, and Baal had more personality and were much more interesting, and their cult offered manifold collateral benefits. It is no wonder that many Israelites, especially in the northern kingdom, were inclined to supplement their worship of their ancestral God with at least a nod in other directions. Divine transcendence has always been a difficult concept to market to ordinary people; many seek a more accessible deity, or at least a tangible image to which they can direct their attention. In a sense, the satires on idolatry in the Psalms and in Second Isaiah are unfair. Just as Jews found focuses for their devotion in the Temple and in the Ark of the Covenant, idols were probably considered no more than visible and tangible points of contact, or portals, into the unseen world of the gods; the points of contact themselves were not seen as divine.

The intimate nature of the divinity remained a mystery. It was through the interventions in the history of the chosen people that the God of Israel was known. These interventions were, in an imperfect sense, the visibility of the invisible God. It was by them that the God of Israel was named (Jer 13:11). The divine nature is revealed by powerful actions taken to liberate the people from the anonymity of slavery in Egypt. The

Feast of the Passover was instituted precisely to ensure that the memory of the events of the exodus was maintained from one generation to the next. The nature of Israel's God was intertwined with Israel's identity as a people. By the middle of the third century BC, however, this memory was crushed by more recent events: the destruction of the northern kingdom by the Assyrians; the deportation of the Judeans to Babylon; and, despite the exaltation that followed the return of the exiles, the struggle to maintain some fragment of national identity as Palestine became the plaything of successive foreign overlords. In such a context, an appeal to God's covenantal loyalty (*chesed*—the term does not appear in Ecclesiastes) was unlikely to provoke the same positive response as hitherto, since the people continued saying, "God is unseeing of our ways" (Jer 12:4). Undoubtedly, many Israelites would wonder whether their ancestral God was still concerned with them. A different approach was necessary.

Religion

We have no comprehensive knowledge of life in Palestine during the third century BC. This is significant in itself. Flourishing cultures usually leave their mark on history, whereas cultures in remission pass by unnoted. The struggle for survival does not leave an impressive footprint. In particular, we do not know a great deal about religious practice during this phase of the Second Temple period. It is probable that, with the collapse of the monarchy, priests assumed some civic responsibilities as well as those associated with the cult. Even though the Ptolemaic hegemony may have been relatively benign, taxes had to be paid to the Egyptian overlords, and those associated with their collection were understandably unpopular. The rise of local synagogues as the mainstay of religious practice, especially in the growing diaspora, initiated a movement of decentralization that reduced the national significance of Temple worship in Jerusalem and, inevitably, opened up the possibility of more pluralism of thought.

Furthermore, suspicion about the authenticity of public worship and its associated rituals had long been a staple of prophetic reproach.[3] The official cult was seen as not always sincere: external worship did not always reflect inner dispositions (cf. Isa 29:13; Jer 12:2; Ezek 33:31), and it often lacked its essential complement—living according to the moral and social demands (*mishpat*) of the *torah*. Qoheleth seems to have been cool toward institutional religion; this is probably because his approach was the conventional one adopted by those who were outside its inner circles. "Qoheleth manifests in 4:17—5:6 (5:1–7) a cautious but reverent attitude to the cult that is not essentially different from the usual critique of cultic abuses."[4] He does not threaten, as Jeremiah does in his temple diatribe (Jer 7:1–15), he simply advises his followers to be somewhat circumspect when they come before God. A hidden God must be served in sobriety; over-enthusiasm is probably an indication of posturing or virtue signaling. If it continued to be true that prophets and priests went about their business, but without knowledge (Jer 14:18), then a certain detachment from official religion was neither irreligious nor unreasonable:

> Take heed to thy foot when thou enterest into the House of God, and be more near to hear than to give

---

3. "It is well known, too, that criticism of the cult was a central element in the denunciations of the pre-exilic prophets." J. Lindblom, *Prophecy in Ancient Israel* (Oxford: Blackwell, 1973), 351.

4. Roland Murphy, *Ecclesiastes* (Dallas: Word Books, 1992), 50.

the sacrifice of fools: for they know not that they do evil. Be not rash with thy mouth, nor let thine heart be hasty to utter a thing before God: for God is in the heavens, and thou art on the earth: therefore let thy words be few. For as a dream cometh by the multitude of business: so the voice of a fool is in the multitude of words. When thou hast vowed a vow to God, defer not to pay it: for he delighteth not in fools: pay therefore that thou hast vowed. It is better that thou shouldest not vow, than that thou shouldest vow and not pay it. Suffer not thy mouth to make thy flesh to sin: neither say, before the Angel, that this is ignorance: wherefore shall God be angry by thy voice, and destroy the work of thine hands? For in the multitude of dreams and vanities are also many words: but fear thou God. (Eccl 4:17—5:6)

Qoheleth admonishes readers to watch their step in entering God's House, to be mindful of the distance that separates the divine sphere (the heavens) from that of humans (the earth). He is warning against the familiarity that is close to contempt: an attitude that is often observed in those involved in the upkeep of sacred spaces or in the mechanics of worship. He is recommending that religious duties be performed mindfully, listening to what is heard, and not offering sacrifice like fools who expect that the rite can be beneficial independent of their interior dispositions. He has observed, in fact, that there is little difference between those who participate in ritual worship and those who omit to do so. The worship of fools is ineffectual, but even the honest piety of the virtuous does not necessarily yield visible benefits. Qoheleth cites another example of unfairness: the wicked receive honorable burial because of their assiduous attendance at the holy place whereas others are forgotten (cf. Eccl 8:10).

All things come alike to all: and the same condition is
to the just and to the wicked, to the good and to the
pure, and to the polluted, and to him that sacrificeth,
and to him that sacrificeth not: as is the good, so is the
sinner, he that sweareth, as he that feareth an oath.
This is evil among all that is done under the sun, that
there is one condition to all. (Eccl 9:3–4)

Those who engage in public worship should act soberly
and reverently. The less they speak the better: "Therefore, let
thy words be few." This restraint of speech is another sign of
reverence before God. "Where there are many words *hevel* is
multiplied. What profit is this to anyone?" (Eccl 6:11). It is
common experience that a multiplicity of words is an indication of a poverty of thought. The empty-headed try to hide
their vapidity behind an overwhelming torrent of words.
They do not have enough sense to work out that their tactic is
counterproductive. Mindless speech is worthless. The more
words the less sense. Their abundance serves no purpose but
to demonstrate that their speaker is a fool. Daily experience
confirms this. "The lips of a fool devour himself. The beginning of the words of his mouth is foolishness, and the latter
end of his mouth is wicked madness. For the fool multiplieth
words" (Eccl 10:12–14). Taking the matter further and draw-
ing from common experience, Qoheleth notes that dreams
tend to multiply when cares increase. Dreams are another expression of *hevel*; they are insubstantial, ineffectual, and mad.

Care in speech is nowhere more important than in the case
of making a commitment to God. In our legal system, oral
agreements carry little weight; we demand documentation.
Verba volant; scripta manent. (Words fly away, but writing is permanent.) In the Semitic world, however, more importance was
attributed to spoken words; in fact, the usual term *dabhar*
means not only a word but, more generally, a thing or deed. In

a sense, any word once uttered was irrevocable, but this was especially so in the case of a vow. Think of the horrific example of Jephthah's impetuous vow which forced him to offer his daughter in sacrifice (cf. Judg 11:30–40). Unfulfilled vows become a target for the divine anger; there is no excuse that will be accepted in mitigation. We have to be careful of what we say: every word is like a promise. The multiplication of dreams and words is an expression of *hevel*; only bad outcomes can be expected of them.

In this relatively short passage we learn something significant about the Preacher. Even though religious practice is not his primary focus, he is not anti-religious. He is aware of the misuses and abuses that occur in the prevailing system, but he does not reject conventional religion itself. He simply regards it as meaningless in the absence of the appropriate interior dispositions. His exhortation to listening locates him within the lineage of the Deuteronomic authors and Jeremiah and, perhaps, reflects the post-exilic shift in Judaism from an emphasis on bloody sacrifices to the more intellectual obligation of hearing the Torah, paying attention to its meaning, and putting its precepts into practice. As for his acceptance of the reality of God, there can be little doubt about that.[5]

Transcendent

We have already seen how Qoheleth reminded his readers that "God is in the heavens, and thou art on the earth." When he describes God as "he that is higher than the highest" (Eccl 5:7),

---

5. It is inaccurate and unfair to describe Ecclesiastes as "the most pagan of the Old Testament books." For this dismissal, see George Cardinal Pell, *Prison Journal: The Cardinal Makes His Appeal* (San Francisco: Ignatius Press, 2020), 1:21.

he is embracing a notion of God that is more metaphysical than historical. He is passing beyond using divine interventions as indicators of God's nature and embracing the notion of a God who is essentially ahistorical. This is also the perspective of the Book of Job. Likewise, the prophet Jeremiah has God ask, "Am I a God who is near, and not a God who is far away?" (Jer 23:23). The idea of transcendence means that an appreciation of the divinity demands a sophisticated level of intelligence. Thomas Aquinas will say that knowledge of God is self-evident—but only to the wise: *per se notum, quoad sapientes tantum*. Byzantine theology will teach that we can understand the works of God which are the effects of the divine energy, but the intimate essence of God is beyond our comprehension. Qoheleth's stance is less developed than this; he simply affirms that understanding what is behind God's activity in our world is beyond us. "Man cannot find out the work that God hath wrought from the beginning even to the end" (Eccl 3:11). God does not work in a single place for a particular time. God's works are spread out over the entire universe of space and time; there is no human being who is able to survey all these activities, since we are confined to a determined place and live for only a brief moment. God's works have been accomplished everywhere from the very beginning and will continue long after we cease to be. If even the works of God are beyond us, by how much more are we unable to grasp what God is:

> Then I beheld the whole work of God, that man cannot find out the work that is wrought under the sun: for the which man laboreth to seek it, and cannot find it: yea, and though the wise man think to know it, he cannot find it. (Eccl 8:17)

Part of the rationale for proclaiming universal *hevel* is that the full uncovering of the meaning of the cosmos is beyond the capability of the human intellect.[6] The unknowability of the earth proclaims the ultimate unknowability of earth's maker. It is a similar argument that the Fourth Gospel attributes to Jesus in his discussion with Nicodemus. "The wind blows where it wills; you hear its voice but you do not know where it comes from or where it goes." Then the corollary, "If you do not believe when I tell you about earthly realities, how will you believe when I tell you about the things of heaven?" (John 3:8, 12). This form of *a fortiori* argument was well known in Jewish tradition.[7] We cannot grasp the whole because many of its parts are beyond our comprehension. Qoheleth gives two examples of our ignorance:

> As thou knowest not which is the way of the [wind], nor how the bones do grow in the womb of her that is with child: so thou knowest not the work of God that worketh all. (Eccl 11:5)

Knowing how much we do not know must surely be at least the beginning of wisdom.

Because we do not know the mind of God, we are not in a position to make credible judgments about the relative value of different events on earth. This is an important element in our acceptance of our reality. We are not obliged to categorize events as positive or negative; we are called to accept what is and to attempt to make the most of what God has given us. Since we do not know the future, we cannot be sure how

---

6. I take the phrase "under the sun" to mean "on earth," perhaps with an added nuance. It occurs twenty-nine times in Qoheleth. I am not convinced by the suggestion that this is a coded reference to Ptolemaic overlordship.

7. See Allen Conan Wiseman, "A Contemporary Examination of the A Fortiori Argument Involving Jewish Traditions" (doctoral dissertation, University of Waterloo, 2010).

things will work out. Surely, it is common experience that something that at first appeared undesirable becomes, with the passage of time, a factor in our future happiness:

> Behold the work of God: for who can make straight that which he hath made crooked? (Eccl 7:13)

We cannot change things, but God can write straight on crooked lines. We have no right to complain about the circumstances that God has allowed to develop around us, because we are unable to assay their real value. There is no need to feel frustration; all we need to do is acknowledge our inborn ignorance and restrict our intellectual searching to those areas where it is possible for us to find answers.

Creator

The affirmation that God is outside the realm of human affairs—"in the heavens" rather than limited to space and time—leads to the recognition that it is from God that the world takes its origin. In his final chapter, Qoheleth admonishes youth to "remember the One who created you" (Eccl 12:1). The reading is not undisputed, but it seems that the Preacher is employing the late term *bara'*, brought into prominence by Second Isaiah and Genesis, a term imbued with a certain theological flavor beyond the meaning of merely making something.[8] This is the only time that Qoheleth uses this verb, but there are other references to God as the maker of all that is:

> [God] hath made everything beautiful in his time: also he hath set the world in their heart, yet man cannot

---

8. See M. Casey, *The Promise of Deliverance: Reading Second Isaiah* (Maryknoll, NY: Orbis Books, 2020), 28–29.

find out the work that God hath wrought from the beginning even to the end. (Eccl 3:11)

The word translated by the Geneva Bible and the ancient versions as "the world," is more often rendered as "eternity" or "duration." The fact that "eternity" is a more abstract notion than Semitic thought would embrace points to the probability that what is meant is that God has placed a sense of duration or permanence in the human heart which stands in contrast to the world of universal change that has just been described (Eccl 3:1–8). In other words, humans stand apart from the world around them, by their capacity to include in their awareness more than the present moment delivers. As we shall see later, this is a mixed blessing.

It is from God that human beings receive the breath of life, and it is to God that this breath must return (Eccl 12:7). Whether humanity's death is different from that of the animals is a moot question:

> I considered in mine heart the state of the children of men that God had purged them: yet to see to, they are in themselves as beasts. For the condition of the children of men, and the condition of beasts are even as one condition unto them. As the one dieth, so dieth the other: for they have all one breath, and there is no excellency of man above the beast: for all is vanity. All go to one place, and all was of the dust, and all shall return to the dust. Who knoweth whether the spirit of man ascend upward, and the spirit of the beast descend downward to the earth? (Eccl 3:17–21)

God has created the human being from the dust of earth but endowed us with special characteristics, among them to walk upright in a world of quadrupeds. "Only lo, this have I found, that God hath made man [upright]" (Eccl 7:29). In Hebrew, as in English, the physical stance of uprightness is often used as an evocation of moral rectitude. According to this text, however, this initial innocence has become vitiated by humanity's pursuit of goals that are alien to its nature: "but they have sought many inventions." What God has given can be frustrated by human willfulness. "The heart of the sons of men is full of evil, and madness is in their hearts while they live" (Eccl 9:3). This is what experience teaches: that God is the origin of all that is, but humans have a role in bringing it to its intended goal; if they are foolish, they can frustrate the plan and bring about their own ultimate unhappiness.

Post-exilic wisdom, in general, is regarded as located "within the framework of a more developed theology of creation." Robert K. Johnston gives some of the connections that exist between Ecclesiastes and the Book of Genesis.

> Thus, Qoheleth recognizes, as does [sic] the Genesis creation accounts, that man is made from the dust and will return to it (Eccl 12:7; 3:20; cf. Gen 2:7; 3:19); that man was meant to live in companionship (Eccl 4:9–12; 9:9; cf. Gen 1:27; 2:21–25); that man is inclined to sin (Eccl 7:29; 8:11; 9:3; cf. Gen 3:1–13); that human knowledge has certain God-given limits (Eccl 8:7; 10:14; cf. Gen 2:17); that life is tiring toil (Eccl 1:3; 2:22; cf. Gen 3:14–19); that death is a great tragedy hanging over mankind (Eccl 9:4–6; 11:8; cf. Gen 3:19, 24; Gen 4); and that God is sovereign (Eccl 3:10–13; cf. Gen 1:28–30; 3:5).
>
> Moreover, Qoheleth is in agreement with the writer of Genesis who viewed the order and regularity of nature as a sign of God's graciousness and blessing (Gen 8:21ff.)....Most importantly, Ecclesiastes and Genesis exhibit substantial agreement as to the central

point of the creation motif—that life is to be celebrated as a "good" creation of God.[9]

It is important to keep in mind this connection because it serves to offset the opinions of those commentators who underestimate the theological context of Qoheleth's philosophy.

Sustainer

Yet in all that transpires on the face of the earth, this God is not inactive. There is a providence at work. "The just, and the wise, and their works are in the hand of God" (Eccl 9:1). The act of creation continues in God's ongoing gifting of the creatures that live their lives within the divine sphere of activity. In fact, in Ecclesiastes, the most common verb associated with God is "give," *nathan* (1:13; 2:26 [bis]; 3:10, 13; 5:17, 18 [bis]; 6:2; 8:15; 9:9; 12:7). Everything that is good in human life is the gift of God—even though it comes to us tinged with the toxin of *hevel*. This is typical of the double-sided reading of reality which we find everywhere in this book. Everything comes from the hand of God and yet, simultaneously, this glorious totality is not solid enough in itself to be taken seriously.

Eating and drinking together with the satisfaction and profit that come from hard work, alongside the possibility of spending time with a loving wife: these are God's principal gifts to humankind. To these fundamental endowments God has added the lesser possibility of acquiring wealth. Those who are good also receive the joy that comes from wisdom and knowledge "but to the sinner he giveth pain," frustration, and vexation of spirit:

---

9. Robert K. Johnston, "'Confessions of a Workaholic': A Reappraisal of Qoheleth," *Catholic Biblical Quarterly* 38, no. 1 (1976): 22.

There is no profit to man: but that he eat, and drink, and delight his soul with the profit of his labor: I saw also this, that it was of the hand of God. For who could eat, and who could haste to outward things more than I? Surely to a man that is good in his sight, God giveth wisdom, and knowledge, and joy: but to the sinner he giveth pain, to gather, and to heap to give to him that is good before God: this is also vanity, and vexation of the spirit. (Eccl 2:24–26)

Those seeking a spiritual message from Qoheleth may be disappointed that he does not propose a loftier ideal. Yet, if everything that comes from the hand of God is good, then the ability to find pleasure in anything that comes from God is an indication that all is well with the person. To enjoy food and drink is the sign of a normal human being. Not to enjoy them suggests that something is wrong. The other components of daily existence, which are also God's gifts, may be harder to appreciate, but if we become wise and develop a positive attitude to all that we encounter in life, then, progressively, everything will become a source of pleasure—even apparent reverses.[10] All the days of our life are lived under the lovingly watchful supervision of God:

Behold then, what I have seen good, that it is comely to eat, and to drink, and to take pleasure in all his labor, wherein he travaileth under the sun, the whole

---

10. Speaking of the petition on the Lord's Prayer that says, "Thy will be done," Saint John Cassian states, "No one can say this prayer sincerely except the one who believes that God disposes everything, whether it seems favorable or not, for our good; and that God watches and cares for our salvation and welfare more than we do ourselves." *Conferences* 9.20; *Sources Chrétiennes* 54, 57–58.

number of the days of his life, which God giveth him: for this is his portion. Also to every man to whom God hath given riches and treasures, and giveth him power to eat thereof, and to take his part, and to enjoy his labor: this is the gift of God. Surely he will not much remember the days of his life, because God answereth to the joy of his heart. (Eccl 5:18–20)

Qoheleth's philosophy of living in the present moment means that one is less inclined to brood over the past or, for that matter, to grieve over the shortness of life. The gift of present joy outweighs both the precariousness of existence and the sadness experienced at other times:

And I praised joy: for there is no goodness to man under the sun, save to eat and to drink and to rejoice: for this is adjoined to his labor, the days of his life that God hath given him under the sun. (Eccl 8:15)

The conclusion must be that we should enjoy the daily pleasures that life offers, for these little episodes of happiness will be a bulwark against future hardship:

Go, eat thy bread with joy, and drink thy wine with a cheerful heart: for God now accepteth thy works. At all times let thy garments be white, and let not oil be lacking upon thine head. Rejoice with the wife whom thou hast loved all the days of the life of thy vanity, which God hath given thee under the sun all the days of thy vanity: for this is thy portion in the life, and in thy travail wherein thou laborest under the sun. (Eccl 9:7–9)

Ultimately, God remains in control of all that happens in this world; it is futile to fret about what is, to be burdened by the past or anxious about the future. It is better to make the most of it and to enjoy life.

Judge

This blithe attitude to life is not irresponsible. The Preacher sets before the reader the prospect of divine judgment. Contrary to received wisdom which advises youth to live as if they were already old, Qoheleth counsels the young to follow, without regret, the dictates of their youthful nature. This is another example of the Preacher's respect for reality: be content to be what you are. It is as though he were saying, "You are only young once. Don't waste your youth." Childhood and youth are evanescent *hevel*; make the most of them before they disappear. He adds that there will be a judgment—so he is not recommending total irresponsibility. All of us are accountable for the choices we make. It has to be said, however, that, given the uncertainty of a future life, the form of divine judgment that he envisaged remains uncertain:

> Rejoice, O young man, in thy youth, and let thine heart cheer thee in the days of thy youth: and walk in the ways of thine heart, and in the sight of thine eyes: but know that for all these things, God will bring thee to judgment. Therefore take away grief out of thine heart, and cause evil to depart from thy flesh: for childhood and youth are vanity. (Eccl 11:9)

The attitude that the Preacher is recommending here is summarized in the phrase "fear God," which conjures up a global attitude of awe, reverence, respect, obedience, and self-restraint. This is the result of appreciating the otherness of God and the inviolability of all the divine works, which human beings are obliged to respect. We are to attune ourselves to reality. This means that, if we are young, we should live our lives youthfully and not pretend to be over-righteous or over-wise. There is a providence even in what seem to be the folly of youth. We live attuned to the reality of who and what we are, accepting its mixity, rather than opting to live in a state of perpetual dudgeon because reality seems unwilling to conform itself to our whims and expectations:

> And also that every man eateth and drinketh, and seeth the commodity of all his labor. This is the gift of God. I know that whatsoever God shall do, it shall be forever: to it can no man add, and from it can none diminish: for God hath done it, that they should fear before him. What is already hath been: and what shall be, hath been before: for God requireth that which is past. And moreover I have seen under the sun the place of judgment, where was wickedness, and the place of justice where was iniquity. I thought in mine heart, God will judge the just and the wicked: for time is there for every purpose and for every work. I considered in mine heart the state of the children of men that God had [tested] them: yet to see that they are in themselves as beasts. (Eccl 3:13–18)

Human beings cannot interfere with the work of God. They need to bear in mind that, in some respects, they are no better than beasts: they cannot change situations that God has ordained. If there is a distortion of justice, God will take note and, at some point, intervene to reverse the disorder. How this will happen is not stated. What comes about through human weakness, blindness, and malice will be repaired and, presumably, the culprits will face some form of sanction. We, however, cannot know how or when this will happen:

If in a country thou seest the oppression of the poor,
and the defrauding of judgment and justice, be not as-
tonished at the matter: for he that is higher than the
highest, regardeth, and there be higher than they.
(Eccl 5:7)

We are admonished to bear in mind that everything is
under control. In God's ordering of the universe, there is a self-
correcting principle. Providence spans both what is good and
what is evil and is able to separate the opposites and deal with
them as they deserve. However, we are unable to determine
the character of what happens around us and there is no guarantee that our efforts to improve what we perceive as a bad situation will yield beneficial results. Perhaps Qoheleth's attitude
is too accepting of our way of looking at things, too passive.
He does not admonish us to take steps to improve a negative
situation but advises us not to be surprised and to be prepared
to endure what (he believes) cannot be changed:

In the day of wealth be of good comfort, and in the
day of affliction consider: God also hath made this
contrary to that, to the intent that man should find
nothing after him. I have seen all things in the days of
my vanity: there is a just man that perisheth in his justice, and there is a wicked man that continueth long in
his malice. (Eccl 7:18)

There is no denying the apparent unfairness of the universe, but the perception of this should not undermine one's
acceptance of what God has given. Fear of God leads to a reverence that does not pass judgment on what God does. Such
an attitude will be to our ultimate advantage. Meanwhile,
those who do not fear God will eventually succumb to the
forces of *hevel*:

Though a sinner do evil a hundred times, and God prolongeth his days, yet I know that it shall be well with them that fear the Lord, and do reverence before him. But it shall not be well to the wicked, neither shall he prolong his days: he shall be like a shadow, because he feareth not before God. (Eccl 8:12–13)

The epilogist caps off the book with the trite injunction "Fear God and keep the commandments," but then attaches a sober warning: "For God will bring every work unto judgment, with every secret thing, whether it be good or evil" (Eccl 12:13–14). This is perhaps a legitimate response to what Qoheleth has written, but it lacks the punch of the rest of the book, which casts the reader into a maelstrom of contrary reasonings about God, the world, and the nature of reality. The Preacher is sure enough that judgment will take place, but he makes no effort to describe its mechanics. The questions he asks are always more important than the answers seemingly contained in the book. It is in the process of questioning and self-questioning that wisdom emerges.

3

WISDOM

The three traditional sources of guidance in Israel were the Torah, effectively administered by the priestly caste, the "word" spoken under inspiration by prophets, and the wisdom accumulated in a lifetime and declared by elders or sages (cf. Jer 18:18). With the decline in the spiritual authority of the priests and the disappearance of the prophets, it was left to the sages to point the way ahead. The age of the Second Temple saw the emergence of Israel's sapiential tradition. The breadth of the concept of wisdom is noted in the opening chapter of the Book of Proverbs:

> For learning about wisdom and instruction,
> for understanding words of insight,
> for gaining instruction in wise dealing,
>   righteousness, justice and equity,
> to teach shrewdness to the simple, knowledge and
>   prudence to the young,
> let the wise also hear and gain in learning
> and the discerning acquire skill to understand a
>   proverb and a figure, the words of the wise and
>   their riddles. (Prov 1:2–6 NRSV-CE)

There are three main components of wisdom: the first is an intellectual grasp of the lessons learned through wide experience; the second is the practical living of these values; the third is competence in communicating them to others. The sage is one who understands, practices, and teaches. What is said and what is done express what the sage is and does. Integrity and undividedness are the hallmarks of those who are wise, and it is their prerogative to teach the young.

There are fifty-one occurrences of the word-family surrounding "wisdom" (*chokhmah*) in Ecclesiastes. The approach taken by its author is nuanced. There is no trace of any notion of the personification of wisdom as is found in other books of Israel's sapiential tradition.[1] A first strand of thought is similar to the Book of Job in that it debunks many of the assertions of conventional wisdom. It acts as criticism of the prevailing ideology, a kind of *Ideologiekritik*.[2] A second strand describes and scorns foolishness in its different manifestations. A third strand praises wisdom and encourages its pursuit. Finally, even while propagating a program to increase wisdom, the book recognizes the limitations of what can be acquired, eventually declaring that it too is subject to the law of *hevel*.

---

1. See Alice Sinnott, *The Personification of Wisdom* (Sydney: Koorong, 2005); Roland Murphy, "The Personification of Wisdom," in *Wisdom in Ancient Israel*, ed. J. Day, R. Gordon, and H. Williamson (Cambridge: Cambridge University Press, 1995), 222–33.

2. Roland Murphy distinguishes between the content of wisdom teaching and its methodology. "Qoheleth is often in conflict with wisdom teaching, but his methodology is nonetheless that of the sage." Murphy, *Ecclesiastes* (Dallas: Word Books, 1992), lxiii. A similar point is made by Rami Shapiro: "Wisdom, then, isn't a body of knowledge but a way of investigating reality and how best to live with it." Shapiro, *Ecclesiastes Annotated and Explained* (Woodstock, VT: SkyLight Paths, 2010), xxxiv.

The style of the Book of Ecclesiastes is a warning against attempting to extract from it a range of definitive statements that may be considered as authoritative wisdom. The book is not intended as a storehouse of wise aphorisms, though many of its sayings are memorable. It is intended to initiate in the reader a recognition of the ultimate questions that are part of the fabric of the cosmos, and to derive from these questions a recognition that there is much in reality that remains puzzling. To ask a question concerning an established belief is to sow a seed of doubt that will, almost certainly, grow. To heap up evidence that contradicts facile assumptions is a dangerous invitation to go deeper, when there is no certainty about the orthodoxy of what is to be discovered in the depths. If we think that such an approach is not constructive, we should remind ourselves that the history of theology signals the fact that development is usually prompted by serious questions being asked. Dull acceptance of what has been received yields no profit. In any field of research, contrarians contribute much to the progress of thought. Creative paradigm shifts are usually initiated by those who were unconvinced by the status quo.

Foolishness

To appreciate wisdom, it is sufficient to observe foolishness in all its varied forms. Saint Jerome remarks that "contrary things are understood by their contraries: the first element in wisdom is to lack stupidity. It is not possible to lack stupidity unless one understands it."[3] A wise person is, perhaps, one who is more fully aware than most of the prevailing idiocy

---

3. *Contrari contrariis intelliguntur, et sapientiae prima est stultitia caruisse. Stultitia autem carere non potest, nisi qui intellexerit eam.* Saint Jerome, *Commentarius in Ecclesiasten, Patrologia Latina* 23; 1075C.

that surrounds us. This bespeaks a reflective and critical attitude toward the world in which we live and move and have our being. And this is the methodology we find Qoheleth following: seeing, reflecting, judging, and then speaking. In his world, as in our own, there was ample evidence to fuel a reflection on foolishness.

There are three word-families that denote this condition of stupidity; it is as though a single word is not enough to cover all the manifestations of this condition.

The term *kesil*, perhaps by association with the fatty parts of the body, means fat, dull, clumsy, or sluggish. It is a term that is used predominantly in the sapiential books. There are eighteen occurrences in Ecclesiastes and forty-nine in the Book of Proverbs. The term is applied to "a young person for whom all attempts at education and training have failed; he acts injudiciously, proves himself foolish and incompetent, and must therefore be disciplined.... When the root is used of reliance on what is worthless, deceptive and ephemeral, it describes a stubborn, defiant, and obstinate persistence in a presumptuous false sense of security and perilous stupidity."[4] As an antonym for "wisdom," *kesil* implies not only intellectual dullness but also practical incompetence and moral deficiency combined with a total lack of self-knowledge and a consequent excess of self-satisfaction: a most unattractive portrait of the depths to which unwise humanity can descend.

The word *siklut* (or *sakal*) is found fourteen times in Ecclesiastes out of an estimated twenty-three occurrences throughout the Old Testament. The Septuagint uses various words to translate it into Greek, and this may be taken as an indication that a perfect equivalent is hard to find. The main idea is that

---

4. Helmer Ringgren, art. "*ksl*," in *Theological Dictionary of the Old Testament VII*, ed. G. Johannes Botterweck et al. (Grand Rapids: Eerdmans, 1995), 267–68.

the fool is one who is not guided by knowledge, whether because he or she lacks the intelligence to acquire it or because they choose to ignore it. If the word includes a sense of "uneducated," it thereby has implications of social class and could be a disdainful reference to the common people, since only the wealthy could afford education.[5]

The third term for foolishness is an alternative use of the root *hll* with the noun *holeloth*, which seems to baffle the experts. Different suggestions are made regarding its distinctive nuance. It seems to involve movement that is haphazard and impetuous and that, in a military context, both evades anticipation and is ineffectual. Perhaps it is like a cat chasing its own tail. Hyperactive stupidity. On the basis of Ugaritic parallels, "moonstruck" has been suggested as a translation.[6]

The study of foolishness is equal in importance to the study of wisdom. They amount to the same thing: both seek to distinguish healthy human behavior from that which diminishes the capacity for life. "I sought in mine heart to give myself to wine, and to lead mine heart in wisdom, and to take hold of folly, till I might see where is that goodness of the children of men, which they enjoy under the sun: the whole number of the days of their life" (Eccl 2:3). The pursuit of wisdom is like degustation of wine—one tastes everything that is available to determine what is best—not by applying abstract criteria, but through personal experience. Observing the foolishness of others is a useful path to self-knowledge, since we are instinctively

---

5. See G. Fleischer, art. "*skl*," in *Theological Dictionary of the Old Testament X*, ed. Johannes Botterweck et al. (Grand Rapids: Eerdmans, 1999), 255–58.

6. See Henri Cazelles, art. "*hll* III," in *Theological Dictionary of the Old Testament III*, ed. G. Johannes Botterweck et al. (Grand Rapids: Eerdmans, 1978), 411–13.

more sensitive in recognizing in others whatever it is that we are unconsciously repressing in ourselves.

The fool can be recognized as he goes about, because he visibly lacks any sense. He does not even know the way to town (Eccl 10:15). He is gauche and does not know how to conduct himself before others (Eccl 6:8), and he is unable to accept advice or correction (Eccl 4:13):

> The heart of a wise man is at his right hand: but the heart of a fool is at his left hand. And also when the fool goeth by the way, his heart faileth, and he telleth unto all that he is a fool. (Eccl 10:3)

Foolishness is obvious to all except those who excel in it. They do not know right from left, and they do not persevere in any course of action but are in a state of constant flux. Unlike the sage, the fool lives his life unseeingly, as in darkness:

> Then I saw that there is profit in wisdom, more than in folly: as the light is more excellent than darkness. For the wise man's eyes are in his head, but the fool walketh in darkness. (Eccl 2:13–14)

The fool lives only for pleasure; work tires him: "The labor of the foolish doth weary him" (Eccl 10:15), and so "the fool foldeth his hands, and eateth up his own flesh" (Eccl 4:5). He is the source of his own ruin. "By slothfulness the roof of the house goeth to decay, and by the idleness of the hands the house droppeth through" (Eccl 10:18). In a world where the material prosperity that follows fruitful labor was considered to be a blessing from God, there was no excuse for indolence. Initiative and industriousness were recommended, even though their reward was neither certain nor immediate. Taking risks was considered part of business. Spending too much time trying to read the future will mean that out of an excess of caution necessary steps are not taken:

> Cast thy bread upon the waters: for after many days thou shalt find it. Give a portion to seven, and also to eight: for thou knowest not what evil shall be upon the earth. If the clouds be full, they will pour forth rain upon the earth: and if the tree do fall toward the South, or toward the North, in the place that the tree falleth, there it shall be. He that observeth the wind shall not sow, and he that regardeth the clouds shall not reap. As thou knowest not which is the way of the [wind], nor how the bones do grow in the womb of her that is with child, so thou knowest not the work of God that worketh all. In the morning sow thy seed, and in the evening let not thine hand rest: for thou knowest not whither shall prosper, this or that, or whether both shall be a like good. Surely the light is a pleasant thing: and it is a good thing to the eyes to see the sun. Though a man live many years, and in them all he rejoice, yet he shall remember the days of darkness, because they are many; all that cometh is vanity. (Eccl 11:1–6)

This proactive approach to life is one that is unknown to the fool, for whom procrastination is second nature. Instead of forging ahead in a rough-and-tumble world, accepting that, in most cases, we have to act on imperfect knowledge, fools do nothing—except to manufacture excuses to legitimate their indolence. Nothing around us is certain, most of our choices have to be based on probability—and probability is best assessed by the wise.

As we have seen, the one activity in which fools excel in diligence is talking. And the more they talk the worse the outcome: they move from stupidity to insanity and, thence, on a slippery path, to wickedness. As the Book of Proverbs states, "In a multitude of words, sin is not lacking" (Prov 10:19):

> The words of the mouth of a wise man have grace: but the lips of a fool devour himself. The beginning of the words of his mouth is foolishness, and the latter end of his mouth is wicked madness. For the fool multiplieth words, saying, Man knoweth not what shall be: and who can tell him what shall be after him? (Eccl 10:11–14)

It is not only the quantity of the fool's speech that is reprehensible; its quality is also to be deplored. A fool has to compensate for the lack of meaning in his words by the volume at which they are spoken. "The words of the wise are more heard in quietness than the [shouts] of him that ruleth among fools" (Eccl 9:17). Fools delight in merrymaking: laughter and singing are their trademarks. The cackling laughter is like the ready crackling of brambles set alight. "A fool lifts up his voice in laughter" (Sir 21:20).

> The heart of the wise is in the house of mourning: but the heart of fools is in the house of mirth. Better it is to hear the rebuke of a wise man, than that a man should hear the song of fools. For like the noise of the thorns under the pot, so is the laughter of the fool: this also is vanity. (Eccl 7:7–8)

But underneath this surface jollity, there is often a seething ocean of resentment and rage, ready to break forth at the slightest provocation. The Preacher adds to his caution about laughter a warning about anger. "Be not thou of a hasty spirit to be angry: for anger resteth in the bosom of fools" (Eccl 7:9). This is an assertion well worth pondering. It seems that the Preacher's experience has led him to the conclusion that foolish chatter often serves to disguise the roiling of hidden resentments. Perhaps this external merriment misleads others; perhaps it also hides from fools the negativity they are feeling. That is why one often observes the sudden plunge from boisterous laughter to towering rage. The observed equanimity of the wise is in contrast to the fool's emotional instability signaled by such volcanic changes.

Foolishness is not just a deplorable quality that is ultimately harmless. It is toxic. It has a corrosive effect on any with whom it comes into contact, and thus has the potential to be the kindling of a collective madness. "Dead flies cause to stink, and putrefy the ointment of the apothecary: so doth a little folly [outweigh] wisdom, and [honor]" (Eccl 10:1). The Preacher goes further. He speaks about "the wickedness of folly, and the foolishness of madness" (Eccl 7:25) to give emphasis to the fact that foolishness implies a moral deficit and not merely cognitive disability. The fool is a sinner (Eccl 9:18), and God "delighteth not in fools" (Eccl 5:5).

> To deal adequately with folly it is essential to recognize it for what it is. This much is certain, it is a moral rather than an intellectual defect. There are men of great intellect who are fools and men of low intellect who are anything but fools.[7]

For Qoheleth, there is more to the notion of foolishness than mere ineptitude in living. There is a willful divorce from reality. The fool's actions are out of sync with the world around him. Such people are determinedly fixed in their private perspective on everything. Because they talk much and listen little, they have no access to the data which could shield them

---

7. Dietrich Bonhoeffer, *Letters and Papers from Prison* (London: Collins, 1953), 139.

from erroneous judgment. The result is that in everything they say or do, they make fools of themselves.

Wisdom

Qoheleth's notion of wisdom is not without an element of paradox. It is, at once, the gift of God (Eccl 2:26) and a goal to be pursued vigorously (Eccl 1:13; 7:25; 8:16). Seeing reality as it is means not only delighting in the beautiful but also taking upon oneself the negativity that is inherent in all that surrounds human existence. The wise are fully in tune with the world in all its ambiguity. Their interior lives mirror the external world; there is also mixity to be found. Neither joy nor sadness are foreign to human experience:

> Behold, I am become great, and excel in wisdom all them that have been before me in Jerusalem: and mine heart hath seen much wisdom and knowledge. And I gave mine heart to know wisdom and knowledge, madness and foolishness: I knew also that this is a vexation of the spirit. For in the multitude of wisdom is much grief: and he that increaseth knowledge, increaseth sorrow. (Eccl 1:16–18)

Human existence alternates between dealing with that which brings happiness and enduring sundry sources of pain. One who is wise acknowledges the reality of both pleasure and suffering. Such a person does not vainly hope to eliminate what is negative, but recognizes it as an integral part of human experience, neither overreacting nor seeking to blame others. Of course, it is always easy to look on the bright side and mindlessly hope for the best, but those who are wise accept life's sober reminders that there will be days of darkness

(Eccl 11:8) and that, in the end, there will be death. That is why the death of our friends often evokes in us salutary thoughts of our own mortality; we ourselves will not be exempt:

> It is better to go to the house of mourning than to go to the house of feasting, because this is the end of all men: and the living shall lay it to his heart. Anger is better than laughter: for by a sad look the heart is made better. The heart of the wise is in the house of mourning: but the heart of fools is in the house of mirth. (Eccl 7:2–4)

Before we reach the mellowness of perfect wisdom, we have to arrive at a good level of maturity that has set aside childish claims to exceptionalism and all sense of entitlement. For every human being, living involves dealing with both good and bad days. Until we accept this truth at the level of feeling, we will not attain even a moderate level of contentment and, as a result, so many things that we encounter on our daily round will cause us grief. If reality constantly disgruntles us, it will seem to others that we have made a preferential option to welcome bad moods.

The hallmark of wisdom is stability, the willingness to persevere in a process while its inevitable contrarieties neutralize each other and a measure of simplicity and harmony is attained. The consequence of such patience is an equanimity that does not short-circuit the process of inquiry but assesses situations reasonably so as to arrive at a realistic interpretation that, in turn, grounds a prudent response. "Who is as the wise man? and who knoweth the interpretation of a thing? The wisdom of a man doth make his face to shine: and the [sternness] of his face shall be changed" (Eccl 8:1). Those who see things as they are in order to adapt themselves to reality are possessed of a certain luminous quality, just as the prejudicial eye and the manipulative attitude render a person unattractive.

"Indeed, the excellence of the knowledge of wisdom giveth life to the possessors thereof" (Eccl 7:14). Those who attempt to hide from reality are forced simultaneously to hide themselves from those around them and, eventually, to withdraw from any profound level of self-knowledge.

Wisdom is such that it is a reliable guide amid the changes and ambiguities of life. It allows us to make choices that are ultimately beneficial and not merely pathways to passing pleasures. "The excellence to direct a thing is wisdom" (Eccl 10:10). It enables us instinctively to distinguish what is good from what is not. When discernment and good judgment become habitual, a strong character that is able to resist unworthy attractions is formed. "Wisdom shall strengthen the wise man more than ten mighty princes that are in the city" (Eccl 7:21). Strength of character is not based on social acceptance and reputation. Positions of prestige and power are no guarantee against foolishness (Eccl 10:6). Wisdom is an interior quality, beyond the reach of external forces. "Then said I, 'Better is wisdom than strength'" (Eccl 9:16). "Better is wisdom than weapons of war" (Eccl 9:18). When the wise speak, there is a persuasiveness about their words that does not depend on any official standing; their words win acceptance on their own merits. "The words of the mouth of a wise man have grace" (Eccl 10:12).

While wisdom is an appropriate target for human endeavor, it is not an easy one. Much experience is required — experience not only of good things but also of what is foolish and evil. It is only by surveying the total ambit of human conduct and seeing for oneself the effect of the choices that are made that one begins to make progress toward the beginnings of wisdom:

All this have I proved by wisdom: I thought "I will be wise," but it went far from me. It is far off, what may it be? And it is a profound deepness, who can find it?

I have compassed about, both I and mine heart to
know and to enquire and to search wisdom, and reason, and to know the wickedness of folly, and the foolishness of madness. (Eccl 7:25–27)

It is depth that characterizes wisdom; "a profound deepness." Wisdom penetrates beneath the surface and is able to perceive that which is hidden from the eyes of folly. Foolish people
live superficial lives; their choices are based on what is easily
perceived, and they never question the implicit conclusions
they draw from rapid observation. The deeper we penetrate the
meaning of things, the longer the journey ahead of us seems.
What wisdom seeks is far distant. In fact, it is the endless seeking that constitutes wisdom. One who claims to have arrived at
wisdom and settles down to enjoy its benefits is a person utterly
submerged in delusion. Self-satisfaction is a key component of
foolishness. Those who believe that they are perfectly capable of
arriving at correct solutions without recourse to others will frequently be proved wrong. This is because broad experience is a
large part of wisdom. It makes sense to take counsel of another
when one's experience is limited. This, no doubt, is why another
wise man has written, "Do all things with counsel and after-
ward you will not be sorry" (Sir 32:24, Vulgate). Wisdom is seeking after meaning. It is a desire for what is beyond one's present
grasp. It is dissatisfaction with what is already possessed. It is
asking questions. It is having doubts. Wisdom is a process, not
a state. The path to wisdom is paved with many reversals of fortune and challenges, and it is by navigating these patiently that
someone begins to arrive at the first foothills of wisdom.

Remembering Death

One of the reminders that impinge frequently on consciousness as we progress toward wisdom is the overwhelming evi-

dence that points to the shortness of life and the inevitability of death, not just as something that happens to others but as our own unavoidable fate. We could even go as far as to assert that mindfulness of death is the beginning of wisdom, a summons to see life as a whole and not be overwhelmed by momentary issues. The ancient Stoics, such as Seneca, Marcus Aurelius, and Epictetus, reminded their disciples to make the most of life with their admonition: *Memento mori* (Remember you must die). Over the door leading to the cemetery in the monastic church at Sept-Fons was inscribed: *Ille hodie, et ego cras* (He [dies] today. I, tomorrow.) And Martin Heidegger characterized human life as a *Sein-zum-Tode* (being-toward-death). It seems that mindfulness of death is a not uncommon theme among philosophers. The consideration of death sets all the events of life in some proportion and it is that perspective which constitutes a large part of wisdom:

> Surely there be many things that increase vanity: and what availeth it man? For who knoweth what is good for man in the life and in the number of the days of the life of his vanity, seeing he maketh them as a shadow? For who can shew unto man what shall be after him under the sun? A good name is better than a good ointment, and the day of death than the day that one is born. It is better to go to the house of mourning than to go to the house of feasting, because this is the end of all men: and the living shall lay it to his heart. (Eccl 6:10—7:3)

For one who loves this earthly life, death must necessarily be bitter (cf. Eccl 7:26), for we cannot know directly what comes afterwards. For each of us, the fact of our death is certain (cf. Eccl 3:2), but its timing is unknown:

> For to every purpose there is a time and judgment, because the misery of man is great upon him. For he

knoweth not that which shall be: for who can tell him
when it shall be? Man is not lord over the spirit to re-
tain the spirit: neither hath he power in the day of
death, nor deliverance in the battle, neither shall
wickedness deliver the possessors thereof. (Eccl 8:6–9)

I returned, and I saw under the sun that the race is not
to the swift, nor the battle to the strong, nor yet bread
to the wise, nor also riches to men of understanding,
neither yet favor to men of knowledge: but time and
chance cometh to them all. For neither doth man know
his time, but as the fishes which are taken in an evil
net, and as the birds that are caught in the snare: so are
the children of men snared in the evil time when it falleth upon them suddenly. And it strikes all alike: good
and wicked, religious and irreligious. (Eccl 9:11–12)

The practice of religion cannot fend off the advent of death,
but all alike are subject to the great equalizer. It does not matter
how spectacular the accoutrements of life have been, in death
all is lost. As for the dead, their preferences and priorities will
cease to be regarded; it is as though they had never existed:

All things come alike to all: and the same condition is
to the just and to the wicked, to the good and to the
pure, and to the polluted, and to him that sacrificeth,
and to him that sacrificeth not: as is the good, so is the
sinner, he that sweareth, as he that feareth an oath.
This is evil among all that is done under the sun, that
there is one condition to all, and also the heart of the
sons of men is full of evil, and madness is in their
hearts while they live, and after that, they go to the
dead. Surely whosoever is joined to all the living,
there is hope: for it is better to a living dog than to a

dead lion. For the living know that they shall die, but the dead know nothing at all: neither have they any more a reward: for their remembrance is forgotten. Also their love, and their hatred, and their envy is now perished, and they have no more portion forever, in all that is done under the sun. (Eccl 9:2–6)

Even the wise cannot escape death, and after they die, they and all their deeds and all their wisdom will vanish from people's minds. "There is no memory of the former, neither shall there be a remembrance of those that shall be later, with them that shall come after" (Eccl 1:11). Note also:

Then I saw that there is profit in wisdom, more than in folly: as the light is more excellent than darkness. For the wise man's eyes are in his head, but the fool walketh in darkness: yet I know also that the same condition falleth to them all. Then I thought in mine heart, It befalleth unto me, as it befalleth to the fool. Why therefore do I then labor to be more wise? And I said in mine heart, that this also is vanity. For there shall be no remembrance of the wise, nor of the fool for ever: for that that now is, in the days to come shall all be forgotten. And how dieth the wise man, as doth the fool? (Eccl 2:13–17)

Once dead, it is as though the person had never been born:

For [a stillborn child] cometh into vanity and goeth into darkness: and his name shall be covered with darkness. Also he hath not seen the sun, nor known it: therefore this hath more rest than the other. And if he had lived a thousand years twice told, and had seen no good, shall not all go to one place? (Eccl 6:6–7)

In fact, in their mortality, human beings are no better than the animals:

> I considered in mine heart the state of the children of men that God had purged them: yet to see to, they are in themselves as beasts. For the condition of the children of men and the condition of beasts are even as one condition unto them. As the one dieth, so dieth the other: for they have all one breath, and there is no excellency of man above the beast: for all is vanity. All go to one place, and all was of the dust, and all shall return to the dust. Who knoweth whether the spirit of man ascend upward, and the spirit of the beast descend downward to the earth? (Eccl 3:18–21)

Death is frustrating because it brings an end to all one's plans and projects; what happens to a person afterwards is beyond that person's control:

> I hated also all my labor, wherein I had travailed under the sun, which I shall leave to the man that shall be after me. And who knoweth whether he shall be wise or foolish? Yet shall he have rule over all my labor, wherein I have travailed, and wherein I have showed myself wise under the sun. This is also vanity. Therefore I went about to make mine heart abhor all the labor wherein I had travailed under the sun. For there is a man whose travail is in wisdom, and in knowledge and in equity: yet to a man that hath not travailed herein, shall he give his portion: this also is vanity and a great grief. (Eccl 2:18–21)

Even a good reputation is precarious; many who were great during their days on earth are quickly forgotten after their death. We depart from this life as we arrived in it—naked:

> As he came forth of his mother's belly, he shall return naked to go as he came, and shall bear away nothing of his labor, which he hath caused to pass by his hand. And this also is an evil sickness that in all points as he came, so shall he go, and what profit hath he that he hath travailed for the wind? (Eccl 5:14–15)

Since there is no possibility of any activity in the region to which the dead pass, whatever needs to be done should be done now. "All that thine hand shall find to do, do it with all thy power: for there is neither work nor invention, nor knowledge, nor wisdom in the grave whither thou goest" (Eccl 9:10). What happens to the person after death is a great unknown. For Qoheleth, there seems to be no other prospect than descent into the underworld of Sheol, together with a loss of personhood commensurate with the dissolution of bodily remains, and the return of the spirit to its source. "And dust return to the earth as it was, and the spirit return to God that gave it" (Eccl 12:7).

The wise person lives with the prospect of death, not as a source of gloom and foreboding, nor as an excuse for inaction, but as an invitation to make the most of the short time available, even though present circumstances seem dire. Remembering death is not sadness or pessimism but rock-solid realism.

Pearls of Wisdom

The epilogue to Ecclesiastes describes Qoheleth as a sage (cf. Eccl 12:9). A careful reading of the book confirms this. He was a wise man, probably of mellower years, from whom most of us can learn something. No doubt every reader will have his or her own favorite aphorisms, but here are a few sayings that, if we were to take them seriously, would probably improve our quality of life:

There is no new thing under the sun. Is there anything, whereof one may say, Behold this is new? it hath been already in the old time that was before us. (Eccl 1:10)

For in the multitude of wisdom is much grief: and he that increaseth knowledge, increaseth sorrow. (Eccl 1:18)

[God] hath made everything beautiful in its time. (Eccl 3:11)

Better is a handful with quietness, than two handfuls with labor and vexation of spirit. (Eccl 4:6)

Two are better than one: for they have better wages for their labor. For if they fall, the one will lift up his fellow: but woe unto him that is alone: [if] he falleth, there is not a second to lift him up. (Eccl 4:9–10)

When goods increase, they are increased that eat them: and what good cometh to the owners thereof, but the beholding thereof with their eyes? The sleep of him that travaileth, is sweet, whether he eat little or much: but the satiety of the rich will not suffer him to sleep. (Eccl 5:10–11)

All the labor of man is for his mouth: yet the soul is not filled. (Eccl 6:7)

Say not thou, Why is it that the former days were better than these? for thou dost not enquire wisely of this thing. (Eccl 7:10)

In the day of wealth be of good comfort, and in the day of affliction consider: God also hath made this contrary to that, to the intent that man should find nothing after him. (Eccl 7:14)

Be not thou just overmuch, neither make thyself over-wise: wherefore shouldest thou be desolate? (Eccl 7:16)

Surely there is no man just on the earth, that doeth good and sinneth not. (Eccl 7:20)

Give not thine heart also to all the words that men speak, lest thou do hear thy servant cursing thee. (Eccl 7:21)

All that thine hand shall find to do, do it with all thy power. (Eccl 9:10)

He that diggeth a pit, shall fall into it, and he that breaketh the hedge, a serpent shall bite him. (Eccl 10:8)

By slothfulness the roof of the house goeth to decay, and by the idleness of the hands the house droppeth through. (Eccl 10:18)

Cast thy bread upon the waters: for after many days thou shalt find it. (Eccl 11:1)

He that observeth the wind, shall not sow, and he that regardeth the clouds, shall not reap. (Eccl 11:4)

Above all, there is the refrain that occurs throughout the book in slightly different forms. In some way, this sentiment could be understood as the key to understanding all that Qoheleth has to teach us:

> And I praised joy: for there is no goodness to man under the sun, save to eat and to drink and to rejoice: for this is adjoined to his labor, the days of his life that God hath given him under the sun. (Eccl 8:15)

Perhaps we might dare to summarize the underlying wisdom that Qoheleth seeks to impart. Be sensible. Learn from experience. Be good. Don't take anything too seriously. Don't be too pleased with yourself. All things are passing. Be prepared for a change of fortune. Have great respect for God's providence and governance, and be prepared to accept cheerfully whatever comes from God's hands. Nothing else matters much. Such is the life of the wise.

4

TIME

In his classic investigation of some of the philosophical issues underlying the Bible, Claude Tresmontant devoted a chapter to the understanding of time. He understood "biblical" thinking as fundamentally evolutionary.[1] This is, of course, a wild generalization. It is true that as messianism became a stronger current in Israel, the view of time and history became more lineal; it was a forward movement toward a goal understood as predetermined by God. But this is not representative of the entire body of biblical texts. The Deuteronomic history, for example, seems to embody the idea that there was progression, but it was in the wrong direction. History was a matter of degradation; things kept getting worse. In contrast to both these outlooks, Qoheleth embraces a circular notion of time. What goes around comes around. The dazzling kaleidoscope of events around us is simply the result of changes occurring within a limited number of components; what appears to be novel is no more than a different way of combining the same elements as before. There is nothing new under the sun.

---

1. Claude Tresmontant, *A Study of Hebrew Thought* (New York: Desclée, 1960), 17–29.

The world around us is not static; it is in constant movement, but the movement is cyclical and, as such, somewhat predictable. Understanding something of the inherent changeability within the stable universe gives us the opportunity to be in tune with the world, ready to change with it, and equally ready to arrive back at our starting point. Change seems immediate, but it is only on the surface. We attain stability by changing in harmony with the world around as it changes, just as surfers stand steady on their boards only by being in harmony with the movement all around them. Underneath everything there is constancy: the constancy of ever-continuing change. Taking everything into account from a broader perspective, there are no surprises. What we learn from present experiences will, if we are wise, enable us to navigate similar situations that will recur in the future. There is nothing new under the sun:

> One generation passeth, and another generation succeedeth: but the earth remaineth forever. The sun riseth, and the sun goeth down, and draweth to his place, where he riseth. The wind goeth toward the South, and compasseth toward the North: the wind goeth round about, and returneth by his circuits. All the rivers go into the sea, yet the sea is not full: for the rivers go unto the place, whence they return, and go. All things are full of labor: man cannot utter it: the eye is not satisfied with seeing, nor the ear filled with hearing. What is it that hath been [in the past], that shall be [in the present]: and what is done [in the present] shall be done [in the future]: and there is no new thing under the sun. Is there anything whereof one may say, Behold this, it is new? It hath been already in the old time that was before us. (Eccl 1:4–10)

A water molecule may seem to have a varied and adventurous life as it is swept downstream into the sea and is thence drawn up as vapor to the clouds, only to come down again as rain. But the cycle just keeps continuing. The sequential variation visible to the superficial observer cloaks the recurring sameness of the process. In the same way, we can be bewildered by the changing cavalcade of life only because we cannot stand far enough back to see its repetitiveness. We cannot perceive the movement of the tide, because we are too busy watching the eddy.

The unchanging substratum of the universe derives from the fact that it is under God's control. Everything acts as it is meant to act, even though we humans are utterly unable to perceive its final purpose or ultimate meaning. Because we do not fully understand why things happen as they do does not mean that they are out of control. It means simply that we are unable to penetrate the transcendent mystery of divine providence. Everything is in motion, but we can perceive only what is present. Its foundational source and its ultimate ending are necessarily beyond our grasp. All human affairs are subject to change but, by God's decree, the earth stands firm forever. Change is not chaos. It occurs within a limited quantum of possibility. Time is not merely a quantitative measure of events; each moment has its particular qualitative significance which, in turn, colors whatever occurs within its embrace:

> When faced with the question of the meaning of the mystery of the passage of time which in its movement is incomprehensible to [us], [Qoheleth] answers, "I know that whatever God does lasts forever; to add to it or subtract from it is impossible. And he has done it in such a way that [we] must feel awe in his presence" (3:14). There is here set down definitively what true

Old Testament faith must never forget, that the world in its every detail is completely dependent on the God before whom [we] must live in reverence.[2]

The challenge for limited human intelligence is to appreciate the "vanity" inherent in our attempts to force the universe to conform to our limited way of seeing things. The universe is directly under God; it matters little whether we understand its ways or approve of them. We are merely part of a larger whole. Our existence is divided into mutually exclusive moments; we pass from one to another. And what is past is irretrievably lost, with only the precarious thread of memory to signal that it ever existed. Our attempts to exercise dominion over the untamable totality are utterly futile. Our claims to understand whatever is happening in the world are a prime example of *hubris*. The best for which we can hope is to understand how limited our understanding is. What God does is not for us to judge; we are to have respect and reverence for what God has disposed. "I know that whatsoever God shall do, it shall be forever: to it can no man add, and from it can none diminish: for God hath done it, that they should fear before him" (Eccl 3:14).

The Dialectic of Time

There is an apparent randomness about human affairs—the rules of cause and effect that we seek to impose upon them do not seem to apply in many cases. "And I saw under the sun that the race is not to the swift, nor the battle to the strong, nor yet bread to the wise, nor also riches to men of understanding, nei-

---

2. Walther Zimmerli, *The Old Testament and the World*, trans. John J. Scullion (London: SPCK, 1976), 51.

ther yet favor to men of knowledge: but time and chance cometh to them all" (Eccl 9:11). Time and chance. But what we regard as a chance occurrence is habitually something of which we do not understand: the interplay of causalities. To us, a man out for a walk who is buried under an avalanche is the victim of a chance event; this is because we do not understand the physics. If we did, we would be able to calculate when the rocks would begin to move and eventually hit the pavement. And if we understood human motivations entirely, we would be able to predict that moment when the man would be where the rocks fell. It is not chance at play; it is our ignorance.

In a well-known passage, Qoheleth makes the point that, in the overarching wisdom of God, the structure of the universe is dialectical. Whereas the being of God is simple and undivided, the world of space and time is compounded of opposites. We may have preferences, but they are irrelevant. Both contrarieties have a divinely ordained function. Human life and human activity are also dialectical. To every reality there is an opposite, and for each there is an appropriate season — "Look on all the works of the Most High thus: two by two, one over against another" (Sir 33:15). Consider this well-known passage from Ecclesiastes:

> To all things there is an appointed time,
> and a time to every purpose under the heaven.
> A time to be born, and a time to die:
> a time to plant, and a time to pluck up that which
> is planted.
> A time to slay, and a time to heal:
> a time to break down, and a time to build.
> A time to weep, and a time to laugh:
> a time to mourn, and a time to dance.
> A time to cast away stones, and a time to gather
> stones:

a time to embrace, and a time to be far from
embracing.
A time to seek, and a time to lose:
a time to keep, and a time to cast away.
A time to rend, and a time to sew:
a time to keep silence, and a time to speak.
A time to love, and a time to hate:
a time of war, and a time of peace. (Eccl 3:1–8)

This poetic passage reads like a refutation of the nineteenth-
century myth of progress—that everything is moving toward a
brighter future. It postulates a world marked by constancy, one
in which contrary elements lead to a sustainable balance; an
earth where there was only birth and no death would quickly
become overpopulated. If we kept everything and threw away
nothing we would be considered pathological hoarders. If we
only spoke and never kept silence, no one would bear to be near
us. And peace is properly appreciated only after a period of war.
It is this *chiaroscuro*—this interplay of light and shade—that
makes life sustainable. The fact that we appreciate one of the
contrarieties more than the other is irrelevant; both are needful.
They are not alternatives. They are complementary.

A similar thought occurred to Marcus Aurelius, and it led
to a similar conclusion. Like the Heraclitean river, everything
is passing; it makes no sense to try to hold on to any one thing
in particular.

One thing hastens into being, another hastens out of
it. Even while a thing is in the act of coming into existence, some part of it has already ceased to be. Flux
and change are for ever renewing the fabric of the
universe, just as the ceaseless sweep of time is for ever
renewing the face of eternity. In such a running river,
where there is no firm foothold, what is there for

[people] to value among all the many things that are racing past them?[3]

The sooner we accept the stable changeability of the created world, the sooner we are likely to become resilient in the face of its necessary vicissitudes. Whether what befalls us seems, at the moment, to be good or bad, we are always able to say, "This too will pass." We can go further and affirm that ultimately what is happening around us is within God's plan for the universe. This is not merely a lazy acceptance of the status quo, but is a springboard for launching ourselves toward the future, confident that hidden within this present moment is ultimate meaning—even if it is not yet discernible by us. The unwanted present is not the beginning of the end but merely a point in a cycle.

The problem is that we underestimate the dynamic potential of each moment. On the one hand, if we are unhappy with the present, we attempt to draw apart from it instead of interacting with it. Or, alternatively, we allow it to submerge us in the sulky slough of despond. On the other hand, if the present moment pleases us, we try to maintain our hold on it, to prevent its moving forward. The cause of our distress is that we do not know enough to evaluate each situation properly, and so we allow ourselves to be unduly disturbed when bad things happen or when good things fade away.

Wise persons are known by the quality of their choices. Those choices, in turn, depend on the accuracy of their reading of situations. Prejudice causes us to dismiss or diminish whatever we do not value so that we see only what we want to see. If the data is incomplete or unbalanced, discernment made on the basis of it will be skewed. Everything that happens has its place within the grand scheme of things, and we

---

3. Marcus Aurelius, *Meditations* 6.15, trans. Maxwell Staniforth, (Harmondsworth: Penguin, 1964), 93.

may not exempt any of it from our assessment. This means that we have to accept the essential mixity of all reality—including our own. As much as we may like to claim a particular adjective to describe ourselves, no single term evokes our total reality, and no quality is entirely untinged by its opposite. As the Preacher reminds us, "Be not thou just overmuch, neither make thy self overwise: wherefore shouldest thou be desolate?" (Eccl 7:16). To accept that we are mostly average—not to say mediocre—is probably a good first step. We cannot see the total picture and, because of our limited vision, we make inadequate decisions and, later, have to pay the price for them. This is not exceptional; it is a normal human situation. Our own mistakes are also part of the fabric of the real world.

As a consequence, we should not allow ourselves to be seduced by lofty dreams of high spirituality when more mundane necessities call out for our attention. We must not attempt to be overrighteous or overwise, nor disconsolate when our feeble efforts fail. This poetic celebration of the variety of times is also a call for moderation and balance in our judgments and in the choices that we make, conscious that any option needs to be complemented by its opposite in order to produce the most fruitful result. We should not push ourselves too far or too fast, even in the demands that we make of our highest powers. We are not pure spirits.

Every moment has its particular nobility and is to be cherished. This is because whatever happens under the sun is ultimately the work of God—no matter how contrary it seems to us. This includes our own choices and, inevitably, our mistakes. Can we believe it? Even those choices that seem to us to be our mistakes have a role to play in the unfolding of God's plan. They are not disasters; they are misunderstood elements in a wider reality. *O felix culpa!* Oh, happy fault!

Surprisingly, perhaps, Qoheleth asserts that the ability to read the signs of the times derives from a faithful response to

God's self-revelation. One who is truly attuned to the mind of the Creator sees that the created world, in all its ambiguity, is indeed very good:

> He that keepeth the commandment, shall know no evil thing, and the heart of the wise shall know the time and judgment. For to every purpose there is a time and judgment, because the misery of man is great upon him. For he knoweth not that which shall be: for who can tell him when it shall be? Man is not lord over the [wind] to retain the [wind]: neither hath he power in the day of death, nor deliverance in the battle, neither shall wickedness deliver the possessors thereof. (Eccl 8:5–9)

We will find from reflecting on our own experience that the best results accrue from a certain lightness of touch. We resist the temptation to become attached to the good times that we presently enjoy and allow ourselves the luxury of being somewhat detached. As for hardship, we endure it with as much grace as we can muster, knowing that eventually it will end. The wise person interacts with present reality but is not conditioned by it. For ourselves, as for others, there is often a grace in interruption. Moments of discontinuity protect us from going stale from sheer repetitiveness. Latent talents emerge when confronted with the unexpected. There may well be some advantage when a desirable situation gives way before something unpleasant; this realization does not make it less painful, but helps us to face it with fortitude and hope.

Seasons

We see a prime example of cyclical recurrence in the yearly seasons, which can serve as a metaphor for the recurrent transitions to which we are summoned in the course of a lifetime. Nothing is more certain than that the seasons will follow each other, even though the exact form that each season takes is different every year, and there is some variation in when the seasons begin and when they end. Meteorologists attempt to forecast the weather by examining the various causative factors as systems emerge. When the cause is understood, the effect can be predicted. But human life is rather more complicated than weather patterns. There are many more causes in play, both objective and subjective, and not all of them are immediate—some draw their energy from events long past.

Our notion of time is conditioned by our reliance on mechanical devices to ascertain at what point in the day we have arrived. To determine duration, we look at the clock. To find out when seasons begin or end, we consult the calendar. Yet in pre-mechanical centuries, times and seasons were reckoned by events. Daybreak occurred when the sun rose or after the cock crowed. For indigenous Australians, the transition between seasons was linked to the behavior of particular plants and animals.[4] The exact dates, according to our calendar, varied from year to year. The seasons do not operate like clockwork: that is why we who watch the calendar become frustrated when they do not conform to our imposed timetables. Seasons function according to their own internal dynamics, which we do not fully understand, and therefore they sometimes surprise us.

---

4. In Victoria, Australia, the six seasons are distinguished thus. Kooyang: the season of eels, late summer (late January to late March). Gwangal Moronn: the season of honey bees, autumn, (late March to June). Chinnup: the season of cockatoos, winter (June to late July). Larneuk: the season of nesting birds, early spring (late July to late August). Petyan: the season of wildflowers, late spring, (late August to mid-November). Ballambar: the season of butterflies, early summer, (mid-November to late January).

There is also variability and unpredictability in human affairs, but we tend to exaggerate their influence, because we are too closely involved to see recurrent patterns. Perhaps also, we are influenced by exclusivist or exceptionalist thinking so that we are dominated by the thought of our particular uniqueness. This is where Qoheleth's teaching can serve a remedial purpose. Yes, we are unique individuals and what we are intimately experiencing at this moment has never been experienced before anywhere in the universe. But, we are also societal animals, and our experiences are mirrored in the lives of others. Furthermore, there are many echoes in the present of what has happened in our lives in times past. There is more than a little déjà vu. We may conclude that, indeed, there is nothing new under the sun.

In the final quadrant of our lives, when Minerva's owl has taken flight, seasonal variation in our previous experience becomes more easily recognizable. This means that we develop greater skill in recognizing the changing moods of our present experience, and in responding appropriately — without regrets and without disproportionate mental confusion. Normal life is not homogeneous; it has its ups and downs, its light and shade, its intermingling of joy and sadness. Many of our problems begin when we try to reduce everything to a repetitive sameness.

Parker Palmer devotes a chapter of his book *Let Your Life Speak*, to exploring the theme of seasons. He writes:

> The notion that our lives are like the eternal cycle of the seasons does not deny the struggle or the joy, the loss or the gain, the darkness or the light, but encourages us to embrace it all — and to find in all of it opportunities for growth.... In the visible world of nature, a great truth is concealed in plain sight: diminishment and beauty, darkness and light, death and life, are not

opposites. They are held together in the paradox of "hidden wholeness."[5]

He believes that our alienation from nature as we move from an agricultural existence to reliance on manufacturing and beyond not only deprives us of an appreciation for the rhythms of the world but leads us deeper into the delusion that we are able to control whatever touches our lives.

> From an early age, we absorb our culture's arrogant conviction that we manufacture everything, reducing the world to mere "raw material" that lacks all value until we impose our designs and labor on it. If we accept the notion that our lives are dependent on an inexorable cycle of seasons, on a play of powers that we can conspire with but never control, we run headlong into a culture that insists, against all evidence, that we can make whatever kind of life we want, whenever we want it. Deeper still, we run headlong into our own egos, which want desperately to believe that we are always in charge. We need to challenge and reform these distortions of culture and ego—reform them toward ways of thinking and doing and being that are rooted in respect for the living ecology of life.[6]

In our willful rejection of life as it is, and our demand that it should conform to our preferences and expectations, we are depriving ourselves of potential sources of personal enrichment. We spend too much energy resisting reality, failing to

---

5. Parker J. Palmer, "There Is a Season," in *Let Your Life Speak: Listening to the Voice of Vocation* (San Francisco: Jossey-Bass, 2000), 95–109. See also the underlying presupposition of Daniel Levinson's study, *The Seasons of a Man's Life* (New York: Random House, 1978).

6. Palmer, "There Is a Season," 97.

recognize that, in the hands of the benign Creator, all things work together for our ultimate welfare. Our lives will be simpler if we accept the reality of seasonal variation and learn how to discern the changing seasons and how to respond most creatively to the inevitable changes which they bring to our experience of life.

A time to cast away, to weep, to die.

You do not have to live long to experience the first onset of an interior winter. No human life is exempt from disappointment, failure, defeat, separation, loneliness, betrayal, depression and, ultimately, death. Winter is the season of subtraction, loss, inactivity, darkness, doubt, and lack of warmth. The great temptation during wintry periods is a loss of hope which we project outside ourselves—all around us, the environment seems to have lost liveliness. It is not always easy to distinguish a dead tree from one that is merely wintering. In the winters of our discontent when everything seems bleak, we tend to presume that the worst outcomes are the likeliest—not only regarding ourselves but also regarding others and the world as a whole.

The second-century *Shepherd of Hermas* describes how, in this age, good people may appear to be indistinguishable from the wicked: both being bare and barren trees. But there is a substantial difference; the wicked are truly dead, but the good are merely wintering. When the season passes, the good will spring back into life. "Just as the trees that shed their leaves in the winter all look alike, with the withered indistinguishable from the living, so too in this age it is not clear who the upright are and who are sinners, but they all appear alike."[7] If others cannot grasp what is happening, it is even less likely that those who are experiencing winter in their own life will appreciate

---

7. Hermas, *The Shepherd*, §52, in *The Apostolic Fathers*, ed. and trans. Bart D. Ehrman (Cambridge: Harvard University Press, 2003), 2:314–15.

that its dominant negativity is contributing something positive. Spurred on by the disapproving glances they find all around them, they will probably blame themselves for their decline in vitality, not appreciating that it is a necessary seasonal stage. What is worse, people enduring such a bleak period often presume that their low assessment of themselves is shared by God. That God loves them less because of their diminished energy. That somehow the experience of winter is not part of God's plan but resistance to it. Here, we need to reflect on the external seasons that we pass through every year. The difference is that personal winters last longer and may have to be endured for years, not months. And it is not always easy to perceive that such periods of dormancy are, in reality, creating a good result. There is nothing unproductive about a field that is left to lie fallow. True, it does not seem to be producing much at the present moment, but this barrenness is in function of an assured fuller fruitfulness in the future. Lying fallow has its own particular integrity:

> Winter invites us to name what is dead in us, to wonder whether it might in fact be dormant—and to ask how we can help it, and ourselves, to "winter through." It can be a powerful experience to realize how much dormancy we contain. As adults we like to pretend that we are complete. If we are willing to drop that pretense and acknowledge all that remains unrealized in our lives, good things may happen, and not just for us.[8]

A person who is in tune with reality knows that there are things that can be easily accomplished at times but are impos-

---

8. Parker Palmer, *A Hidden Wholeness: The Journey toward an Undivided Life: Welcoming the Soul and Weaving Community in a Wounded World* (San Francisco: Jossey-Bass, 2004), 82.

sible to accomplish during winter. As Saint Bernard remarks, "As with everything under heaven, not every time is suitable and appropriate for this work."[9] He continues:

> He knew that the time of pruning had not yet come and that there would be no response from the vines for his hard work. Why was this? Because in the hearts of those without faith it was still winter. The winter squalls of malice still covered the earth and were more likely to wash away the seeds of the Word than to nurture their growth and so bring to nothing the cultivation of the vines.[10]

Most of us suffer from impatience; once we decide on a project we are reluctant to allow it to proceed at its natural pace. We want to hurry it along. Precipitate progress often threatens the achievement of a goal. If you want to cook a perfect sponge cake, don't open the oven prematurely. Wisdom knows when to wait. If the present is bad, it can only get better. In winter, we learn to appreciate the wisdom of waiting.

A time be born, to heal, to gather stones.
Unbelievable though it may have seemed previously, winter eventually gives way to spring. What once appeared to be dead now shows signs of new life:

> For now the winter is past, the rain is over and gone. The flowers appear on the earth: the time of singing has come, and the voice of the turtledove is heard in

---

9. Bernard of Clairvaux, *Sermones super Cantica Canticorum* (SC) 58.4; *Sancti Bernardi Opera* (Rome: Editiones Cistercienses, 1957–1978), 2:129.

10. Bernard of Clairvaux, SC 58.6; *Sancti Bernardi Opera* 2:130–31.

our land. The fig tree puts forth its figs, and the vines are in blossom; they give forth fragrance. Arise my love, my fair one, and come away. (Song 2:11–13)

The period of aggressive dormancy eases and is replaced by the tentativeness of change, though there are still recurrent spells of bleakness. But there are small signs of hope. The hours of daylight seem longer and stronger. It becomes clearer that the purpose of darkness and doubt was to extinguish false certainties; the distress caused by apparent decline operated in the service of a purer truth. "In the spiritual life disillusionment is a good thing: it means losing our illusions about ourselves and each other. As those illusions fall away we will be able to see reality and truth more clearly."[11] As the urgency of crisis passes, we notice that we have been liberated from a multitude of superfluous dogmas and self-imposed obligations. Like leaves that have served their purpose, they have fallen away and left us bare. Our faith is now less bound up with the details of creedal doctrine; it is experienced more as a mysterious attachment that transcends analytic definition, and becomes more and more infused with an interpersonal character. From being an acceptance of historically conditioned propositions, it moves deeper into the experience of "I-Thou." In the language of the Fourth Gospel, "believing" becomes "believing-in." Strangely, this barer hope feels firmer than it ever felt when it was more expansively arrayed. And lighter too, because it is suffused with the uplifting vigor of hope.

This season of rebirth is a time of emergent freedom. The future no longer seems fixed within rigid boundaries but now appears gloriously open. We feel empowered to reach out and touch what we have never fully encountered before. Tentative-

---

11. Parker Palmer, "On Staying at the Table: A Spirituality of Community," six.eight.org, accessed on December 18, 2020.

ness progressively gives way to boldness, and before we know it, we are being transformed by our purposeful moving into unexplored territories. Slowly a smile begins to take up a more permanent residence on our faces.

A time to laugh, to dance, to love.
The promise afforded by spring is not deceptive. Summer is a time of visible growth; it is the season of abundance and exuberance. No sense of precariousness remains. We begin to recognize and accept our latent abilities and, with great optimism, seek occasions to employ these talents.

> In summer, it is hard to remember that we had ever doubted the natural process, had ever ceded death the last word, had ever lost faith in the powers of new life. Summer is a reminder that our faith is not nearly as strong as the things we profess to have faith in—a reminder that for this single season, at least, we might cease our anxious machinations and give ourselves to the abiding and abundant grace of our common life.[12]

Summer allows us to become a closer embodiment of what we are meant to be, and this is something recognized not only by ourselves but also by all with whom we come into contact. So delighted are we with this change in our situation that there is a danger that we will become so self-congratulatory that we forget that not everyone is passing through a stage of exultant abundance. This is where we need to become aware that the many gifts of which we are the beneficiaries summon us to share with others what we have received, to exert ourselves so that these gifts may somehow touch and renew others in addition to ourselves. What we have been

---

12. Palmer, *Let Your Life Speak*, 109.

given is not for ourselves alone; it is amplified when it is used to enrich the lives of others.

A time to sew, to plant, to build.
When life is full, it tends to overflow. Simply to be alive seems insufficient. Fullness of life must become life-giving. It cannot be complete unless it is generative. Inevitably, whatever is created bears the imprint of the ones who made it and, thus, expands their influence beyond the limits of their own limited lifespan. The epitaph given to Sir Christopher Wren, the architect of St. Paul's Cathedral in London, is true of us all: "If you seek a memorial, look around you." What we have done survives us. It is like an extension of ourselves. Generating this extension is one of the most fulfilling experiences we can have; we feel fully alive. Everything that we have previously experienced seems to come to fruition at this time, and we hope and believe that it will continue indefinitely. But we should know better.

For there are clouds on the horizon. There are two unseen dangers lurking beyond the edges of our elation. The first is that we will become arrogant, assigning to ourselves all the credit due to our successful ventures, not only forgetting that we are the beneficiaries of God's generosity but also undervaluing the direct and indirect contributions of many others and, as well, underestimating the role played by what may be termed "good luck." The second danger is that we so enjoy making the most of our talents that we lose sight of our limitations and overextend ourselves. The result is burnout. We reach a point at which we no longer feel stimulated by what we do, our freshness and verve wane, and we begin to doubt that we have anything else to give. Perhaps we dismiss what we had previously accomplished as worthless. "All is vanity." The season has done its work. It is time for a change.

Where the weed of arrogance has grown, it must be uprooted. This will be the task as a new winter approaches, clearing the ground of unwelcome growth and returning the soil to a more receptive state. It is no accident that the word "humility" derives from the word for soil, *humus*. We have to come down from the heights of success to be re-grounded in the vulnerability of our humanity. Even when we accomplish much, we are not gods; at best, we are agents of a more powerful but unseen energy. We have to relearn our limits. Winter forces us to endure a time of inactivity and waiting, powerless to do much to remedy our deadness.

Life that pours itself out soon finds itself empty. The exhilaration resulting from successful activities cloaks the need for rest, relaxation, recuperation, and even re-creation. We allow ourselves to be drawn into more and more projects, not all of which repay our expenditure of effort. Exhaustion follows and, before long, we find ourselves incapacitated and the victims of self-disgust. Our season of mellow fruitfulness gives way before a barer landscape that gives no sign of ever coming to an end.

Sometimes our experience of winter is precipitated or intensified by others who are envious of our visible accomplishments and anxious to cut us down to size. Under one pretext or another, they block our opportunities to exercise our talents, inhibit our contact with those who offer us support and affirmation, and work hard to ensure our reputation is sullied. Read the biographies of men and women who lived close to God; you will not find many who were spared some level of persecution, not only by the wicked but, more usually, also by the good. So many founders of religious institutes were eventually rejected by the very group for which they had labored so sincerely in years past. In such situations, there is no alternative but to hunker down in the hope that this misfortune is somehow located within the parameters of Providence, and it also shall pass.

And so it does; and the cycle begins anew.

When I view my life through the prism of seasonal varia-tion, I find that much of what I have experienced begins to make sense. Perhaps this is what Qoheleth was trying to teach us. No one season is better than another; they all have a task to accomplish. None of them is inessential. I can look back on my past with at least a glimmer of understanding. As for the pres-ent, I have learned to step back and take time to consider the season that I am in at this moment and what tasks I need to un-dertake to ensure that my time is well spent. This means that I regard all the seasons of my life as coming from the hands of God, as precious gifts: opportunities to move toward a more abundant life—but opportunities that must be seized now, lest they vanish forever. As Parker Palmer reminds us:

> The notion that our lives are like the eternal cycle of the seasons does not deny the struggle or the joy, the loss or the gain, the darkness or the light, but encour-ages us to embrace it all—and to find in all of it oppor-tunities for growth.[13]

For many of us, reflecting on the nature of time may seem too much like abstract philosophy.[14] Yet Qoheleth's approach is

---

13. Palmer, *Let Your Life Speak*, 96.

14. Saint Augustine's bafflement is well known. "For what is time? Who could find any quick or easy answer to that? Who could even grasp it in his thought clearly enough to put the matter into words? Yet is there anything to which we refer in conversation with more familiarity, any matter of more common experience, than time? And we know perfectly well what we mean when we speak of it, and understand just as well when we hear someone refer to it. What, then, is time? If no one asks me, I know; if I want to explain it to someone who asks me, I do not know." *Confessions* 11, 17. *The Confessions of St. Augustine*, trans. Maria Boulding (London: Hodder & Stoughton, 1997), 295.

easy to understand. He fills time with experiences and creates, as it were, human time. There is variation in times and there is variation in experiences. Each alternating facet is God's work. Each has a function to accomplish. No single moment is normative, but there is a special purpose for all of them, "For to every purpose there is a time and judgment" (Eccl 8:6).

What all this means in practice is the adoption of a stance of equanimity. Wisdom is expressed by evenness of mood in a changing world so that we can respond to what is happening around us, rather than thoughtlessly reacting to it or mindlessly remaining unmoved, locked in the delusion of eternal sameness. Changing our outlook to suit the changing circumstances is based on faith in Providence. Paradoxically, even our willingness to keep changing mirrors the constancy of God, maintaining a straight course amid the swirls of an ever-changing sea. Such is the course recommended by the twelfth-century Cistercian Isaac of Stella to his fellow monks:

> My dear friends, this is a good peace and a tranquility of heart: to maintain oneself in evenness of disposition, and to listen with reverence to everything that takes place under heaven. To bless God in everything, for it is God who arranges everything. Not to will to change anything, for it has been well done and contributes to the beauty of the whole. To maintain charity in all situations, the charity which—as it is said—does not rejoice in evil, but rejoices in the truth.[15]

---

15. Isaac of Stella, *Sermons* 47.20; *Sources Chrétiennes* 339, 150.

5

HARD TIMES

If we have a sound philosophy of life, it will serve as a bulwark against the tribulations that inevitably puncture our progress. This is the point that Boethius (477–524) was making when he wrote *The Consolation of Philosophy*, seeing philosophy as a nurse, caring for us when we are struck down by the strokes of unavoidable misfortune. Medieval writers often spoke of human life as characterized by *miseria*. By this term they did not mean the subjective state of misery and unhappiness as much as the objective condition of unavoidable suffering, beginning at birth and terminating only at death. Saint Aelred of Rievaulx defines the word succinctly, "Pertaining to *miseria* are all the miseries of this life: labors, pains, weariness, poverty, bereavement, all types of illness, trouble. O my brothers, who can number them all?"[1] If we accept that suffering is an inevitable part of the landscape of human life, it will be much easier for us to cope with hardship when we experience it. Such acceptance does not reduce the pain itself, but it diminishes the level of mental confusion; this is all part of what it means to be human.

---

1. Aelred of Rievaulx, *Sermones* 43.13; *Corpus Christianorum Continuatio Mediaevalis* 2a, 339.

It is typical of reality that bad things happen to good people as well as the wicked. Eastern European philosophers, like E. M. Cioran, by dint of long experience, are better at incorporating pain into their worldview than the thinkers of the West. Those who have been brainwashed by the happy-face philosophy of Disneyland are habitually imbued with a sense of entitlement that makes them think that the pursuit and attainment of happiness are theirs by right. Suffering is for other people; they consider themselves to be exceptions to its universal claim. This means that when hard times come, they suffer the additional affliction of interior anguish: instead of coping practically with the trouble and trying to minimize its impact, they complain and eventually move into an aggrieved sense of victimhood, and thence into seeking someone to blame for their situation. Often, this leads to ongoing litigation to assuage their wounded rights by punishing someone else. Since they have excluded the merest possibility of complicity in their own misfortune, they never come to grips with reality and, as a result, their unresolved grievance remains a thorn in their side for years to come. Instead of moving on, their onward march is bedeviled by their being stuck in a mournful morass of their own making.

Qoheleth, as a realistic observer of human experience, did not exclude the negative from his purview. He did not think of suffering as a punishment for wrongdoing, but understood that our universe is a necessary mixture of positive and negative. Our days are full of pain and grief (cf. Eccl 2:23) so that sometimes we are prone to despair (cf. Eccl 2:20). Oppression is endemic, especially for the poor (cf. Eccl 5:8). Wickedness is found in the place of judgment (cf. Eccl 3:17). Fools are promoted beyond their competence (cf. Eccl 10:4–7). Officials are corrupt (cf. Eccl 5:8). Those who rule us are incompetent (cf. Eccl 4:13). Extortion and bribery are rampant (cf. Eccl 7:7). The good perish while the wicked seem to flourish (cf. Eccl 7:15), and the righteous receive what the wicked deserve (cf. Eccl 8:14). "This is evil among all that is done under the sun, that there is one condition to all, and also the heart of the sons of men is full of evil, and madness is in their hearts while they live, and after that, they go to the dead" (Eccl 9:3). The days of darkness are many (cf. Eccl 11:8). Qoheleth's conclusion is that perhaps we are better off dead—even though elsewhere he states that he would prefer to be a living dog rather than a dead lion (cf. Eccl 9:3). The inevitable misery is compounded by the absence of comforters:

> So I turned and considered all the oppressions that are wrought under the sun, and beheld the tears of the oppressed, and none comforteth them: and lo, the strength is of the hand of them that oppress them, and none comforteth them. Wherefore I praised the dead which now are dead, above the living, which are yet alive. And I count him better than them both, which hath not yet been: for he hath not seen the evil works which are wrought under the sun. (Eccl 4:1–2)

The picture he draws is grim, but his approach is descriptive rather than evaluative. He simply says this is the way things are. His unspoken admonition is, "Get used to it. It is not likely to change any time soon." He is viewing the world objectively, as a first stage in formulating suggestions on how to respond to its challenges. As long as we are in denial about the world around us, we will be unable to determine how best to make the most of present circumstances and, perhaps, how to find happiness and to effect some improvement. Inevitably, there will be times when we think that Qoheleth's negativity is exaggerated. There will also be times when we may conclude that the evil and misery of the world are greater than he envisaged. In either case, the point he is making remains valid. Our world is a mixture of good things and bad; our experience of it will alternate between happiness and sadness.

Suffering is par for the course. It is foolish to think that we alone have to endure hard times and fail to recognize that such is the lot of all humankind. The specifics may be particular to our particular circumstances, but the fact of suffering is universal. "Say not thou, Why is it that the former days were better than these? For thou dost not enquire wisely of this thing" (Eccl 7:10). Saint Augustine was of the same mind:

> What fresh sort of suffering, my friends, does the human race now endure that our ancestors did not undergo? Or when do we endure the kind of sufferings which we know they endured? Yet you find people complaining about the times in which they live, saying that our parents' times were good. What if they could be taken back to the times of their parents? Would they still complain? The past times that you think were good are good only because, in the here and now, they are not yours.[2]

Good times and bad times. Both come from the hand of God. Each serves a purpose, unknown to us, but we are called to accept in faith that whatever comes by Providence will be ultimately benign. To attain to this confidence, we have to stop making rapid judgments on the present situation, recognizing that, due to our limitations, the whole story is hidden from us. Forming an assessment on the basis of only a part of the evidence is a surefire recipe for making a mistake:

---

2. Saint Augustine, *On the Anguish and Trials of This Time* 2.92; *Patrologia Latina, Supplementum* 2, 441–42. Augustine's generation was, of course, traumatized by the so-called Sack of Rome by Alaric and his Visigoths (410 AD).

Behold the work of God: for who can make straight that which he hath made crooked? In the day of wealth be of good comfort, and in the day of affliction consider: God also hath made this contrary to that, to the intent that man should [discover] nothing [about the future]. (Eccl 7:13–14)

Toil

Both the "P" (Priestly) and "J" (Yahwist) traditions of the Pentateuch represented in the Genesis accounts of human creation understand work to be a normal element of life in Paradise (Gen 1:28; 2:15). It is only after the primal act of disobedience that work becomes both laborious and fruitless (Gen 3:17–19). Work remains an integral part of our human existence, but in these postlapsarian times, work demands a greater expenditure of energy and effort (the sweat of our foreheads) and often does not yield the outcome we had intended. These negative outcomes are often linked. The work seems hard when it is not producing the results for which we had hoped. However, no effort is spared in the completion of a visibly successful task.

Qoheleth uses the word *'amal* (toil) and its cognates thirty-five times in the course of his book, almost half of the word's occurrences in the Old Testament. Elsewhere the word is translated variously as "oppression" (Deut 26:7), "trouble" (Job 3:10; 5:6), "mischief" (Job 4:8; Ps 140:10), "weariness" (Ps 73:16), and "sorrow" (Jer 20:18). The theme is particularly common in wisdom literature, generally with a strong negative connotation, often as shorthand for the hardship inherent in human existence. In Ecclesiastes, the term is largely neutral; it mostly signifies work in general, although sometimes there is particular emphasis on its toilsome and frustrating components. These negativities derive from the fact that the desired outcome or profit (*yitron*) of any task is by no means certain, dependent as that outcome or profit is on many external factors. When work is merely a means to an end beyond itself, its value is necessarily precarious. Work is good only to the extent that it produces the anticipated result. If it does not, then it is regarded negatively. It is not work itself which is deemed hard, but the fact that it is so often fruitless. When the outcome is certain, no effort is spared in its pursuit.

Work is an inalienable part of human life and, as such, it shares its joys and sorrows. In particular, it falls under the law of *hevel*. For all his industry, the worker has little impact on the world or even on his immediate environment: "What remaineth unto man in all his travail, which he suffereth under the sun? One generation passeth, and another generation succeedeth: but the earth remaineth forever" (Eccl 1:3–4); "What profit hath he that worketh of the thing wherein he travaileth?" (Eccl 3:9). We cannot change the reality around us and, in any case, what we think we have created will soon pass into the hands of those who have no great concern about what happens to the fruit of our labor.

> I hated also all my labor, wherein I had travailed under the sun, which I shall leave to the man that shall be after me. And who knoweth whether he shall be wise or foolish? Yet shall he have rule over all my labor, wherein I have travailed, and wherein I have shewed myself wise under the sun. This is also vanity. Therefore I went about to make mine heart abhor all the labor wherein I had travailed under the sun. For there is a man whose travail is in wisdom, and in knowledge and in equity: yet to a man that hath not travailed herein, shall he give his portion: this also is vanity and a great grief. For what hath man of all his travail and grief of his heart, wherein he hath travailed

under the sun? For all his days are sorrow, and his travail grief: his heart also taketh not rest in the night:
which also is vanity. (Eccl 2:18–23)

People bestir themselves to engage in activity only because they are positively moved to do so; otherwise they
would spend their lifetimes dozing like lizards in the sun.
They are driven to work by their needs and their desires. Yet
even when these immediate urgings are satisfied, their needi-
ness remains and their desire is unfulfilled. They are driven to
work harder. "All the labor of man is for his mouth: yet the
soul is not filled" (Eccl 6:7). The strange thing about humans
that we do not observe in animals is that work is often discon-
nected from our physical needs; it is driven by impulsions
coming from within. As a result, it is not unknown that people
work to excess—even though what they are doing is demanding and wearisome. They condemn themselves to greater toil
to appease some inner demon driving them to ever-greater effort. This is no recent phenomenon; it is described accurately
by Saint John Cassian, a fifth-century monastic writer in the
tradition of the Desert Fathers:

> A certain very experienced elder once happened to be
> passing by the cell of a brother who was afflicted by an
> illness of soul which caused him to toil at constructing
> and repairing buildings every day, far beyond what
> was necessary. From a distance the elder watched him
> breaking hard rock with a heavy hammer. Then he no-
> ticed an Ethiopian standing beside him also grasping
> the hammer as he hit the rock, and who kept urging
> him with fiery promptings to work harder.
>
> The elder stood still for a long while, amazed at
> the sight of such a baleful demon and at the extent of
> the deception being inflicted. When the brother be-

came tired and had no energy left and wanted to stop work and rest, then, at the prompting of this spirit, he was persuaded to take up the hammer again, and encouraged not to desist from what he had intended to do when he began. The brother was so moved by these urgings that his tiredness left him. So he resumed his heavy labor, and yet felt no pain.

The elder was so disturbed by this performance on the part of the dread demon that he turned aside to the brother's cell and greeted him. He asked: "Brother, what is this work that you are doing?" The brother answered, "We are working on this very hard rock, and it is only with great difficulty that we are able to make any impression on it." At this the old man replied, "It is well that you say 'We are working,' since you are not alone when you are working on this rock. There was another with you whom you did not see who has been less a helper than a most oppressive taskmaster in this work."[3]

This story is a reminder that what makes work a burden is not its inherent quality but what is superadded to it or superimposed on it. When the worker is in harmony with the task, it is done with "flow."[4] Whenever work is done at the behest of a taskmaster, it is oppressive and causes resentment. In like

---

3. John Cassian, *Conferences* 9.6; with apologies to the people of Ethiopia.

4. In 1990, Mihaly Csikszentmihalyi wrote *Flow: The Psychology of Optimal Experience* (New York: Harper and Row, 1990), where he introduced a new term into the language. The optimal experiences about which he wrote were moments in which persons are substantially free of outside pressure and able to concentrate fully on what they are doing, not anxiously but with a sense of delight. So close is the identification of the doer and the deed that it is almost as though the activity performs itself. It flows.

manner, when work is done under the tyranny of the super-ego, driven by ambition, perfectionism, or some other sub-personal motivation, it loses its inherent dignity and becomes the tool of dubious inner demons.

The fool adds to his labors by his inability to gauge the purpose of his toil and to respond to it proportionately. "The labor of the foolish doth weary him: for he knoweth not to go into the city" (Eccl 10:15). Because he lacks the common sense to perform ordinary tasks, the fool finds the simplest works difficult and burdensome. He would much rather do nothing. Idleness becomes a besetting fault. "By slothfulness the roof of the house goeth to decay, and by the idleness of the hands the house droppeth through" (Eccl 10:18). Idleness achieves nothing and is ultimately self-destructive. "The fool foldeth his hands, and eateth up his own flesh" (Eccl 4:6).

The effect of unloved labor is an ongoing state of discontent and exasperation. The word used seven times by Qoheleth is *ka'as*. The complex meaning of the word is demonstrated by its being translated by the NRSV in various ways: sorrow, anger, vexation, anxiety. It is probably best considered to be a combination of all of these—a state of being in a permanent bad mood. "For what hath man of all his travail (*'amal*) and grief of his heart, wherein he hath travailed under the sun? For all his days are sorrow, and his travail grief (*ka'as*): his heart also taketh not rest in the night: which also is vanity" (Eccl 2:23–24). It is not the work itself that is the source of negativity, but ulterior motivations such as ambition, envy, or competitiveness that render it contentious. "I beheld all travail, and all perfection of works that this is the envy of a man against his neighbor: this also is vanity and vexation of spirit" (Eccl 4:4).

The quality of work is more important than its product. "Better is a handful with quietness, than two handfuls with labor and vexation of spirit" (Eccl 4:7). This involves working mindfully, concentrating on the doing of the task rather than dreaming of the secondary benefits that will accrue from its realization. This means having a concern to do everything well, irrespective of the extrinsic value attributed to the task. Placing all their hopes only on external results is pointless because, soon enough, the workers will be dead and unable to enjoy whatever fruits their efforts yield:

> As he came forth of his mother's belly, he shall return naked; to go as he came, and shall bear away nothing of his labor, which he hath caused to pass by his hand. And this also is an evil sickness, that in all points as he came, so shall he go, and what profit hath he that he hath travailed for the wind? (Eccl 5:14–15)

Yet, work that is proportionate to one's strength and made meaningful by its purpose is not a burden. For those who are wise, work is its own reward. "I withdrew not mine heart from any joy: for my heart rejoiced in all my labor: and this was my portion of all my travail" (Eccl 2:10). Its intrinsic quality is not dependent on the approval of others nor, to some extent, on its correspondence to the worker's expectations. Even if the outcome is technically a failure, the activity of working can still be profitable and pleasurable. The moment of working is complete in itself as long as the worker is fully present to the task. Fulfilling work is seen as the gift of God. Not to have work to do is to be accursed:

> There is no profit to man: but that he eat, and drink, and delight his soul with the profit of his labor: I saw also this, that it was of the hand of God. (Eccl 2:24)

The animal functions of eating and drinking are conjoined with fruitful labor as the essential occupations of the human being. All alike are ultimately empowered by God and must be viewed as gifts of God. Not to enjoy them is a deformation of nature and, as such, a source of alienation from God. They become the tools of sin. Normally, there is something seriously wrong with a person who does not enjoy eating and drinking. And the same is true of working, for who does not feel a certain exhilaration when a task is completed—even if it is only relief that the labor has ended?

> I know that there is nothing good in them, but to rejoice, and to do good in his life. And also that every man eateth and drinketh, and seeth the commodity of all his labor. This is the gift of God. (Eccl 3:12–13)

We find, here, a summary of Qoheleth's philosophy of life: rejoice and do good, because our lives are a gift from God. To live life to the full, without being distracted by either past or future, involves a willingness to see whatever happens in the present as coming from the hand of God and, as a result, not wishing things to be otherwise. And, in dark days, not allowing the negativity of the moment engulf our underlying joy at being alive.

> Behold then, what I have seen good, that it is comely to eat, and to drink, and to take pleasure in all his labor, wherein he travaileth under the sun, the whole number of the days of his life, which God giveth him: for this is his portion. Also to every man to whom God hath given riches and treasures, and giveth him power to eat thereof, and to take his part, and to enjoy his labor: this is the gift of God. Surely he will not much remember the days of his life, because God answereth to the joy of his heart. (Eccl 5:17–19)

There is a theological dimension to the evenness of disposition that Qoheleth regards as the ideal. Everything that comes from the hand of God is necessarily good. If we are unable to perceive that this is so in our present circumstances, then this is due to deficient perceptiveness on our part. This is a principle clearly enunciated by Saint Augustine: "Let him judge that whatever seems to him to sound absurd is rather something that he is unable to understand, and that there is something great hidden there."[5] That even the wisest among us cannot always ascertain the appropriateness of God's action says something about us and nothing about God. "Then I beheld the whole work of God, that man cannot find out the work that is wrought under the sun: for the which man laboreth to seek it, and cannot find it: yea, and though the wise man think to know it, he cannot find it" (Eccl 8:17). Toil is an integral part of human existence and those who engage in it as part of their lot or portion (*cheleq*) are right to find satisfaction in it. "Therefore I see that there is nothing better than that a man should rejoice in his [works], because that is his portion" (Eccl 3:22; see also Eccl 5:18; 9:9).

When work is done in solidarity with others, any inherent frustration is reduced and a possibility exists of solving any problems that may arise. There are hidden dangers in even the simplest of tasks that strike unexpectedly and catch us unprepared: "He that diggeth a pit shall fall into it, and he that breaketh the hedge, a serpent shall bite him. He that removeth stones shall hurt himself thereby, and he that cutteth wood shall be in danger thereby" (Eccl 10:8–9). It is better to work with others than to toil alone:

> Again I returned, and saw vanity under the sun. There is one alone, and there is not a second, which hath neither son nor brother, yet is there no end of all his travail,

---

5. Saint Augustine, *On Psalm 118* 31, 5; *Corpus Christianorum* 40, 1772.

neither can his eye be satisfied with riches: neither doth he think, "For whom do I travail and defraud my soul of pleasure?" This also is vanity, and this is an evil travail. Two are better than one: for they have a better [outcome] for their labor. For if they fall, the one will lift up his fellow: but woe unto him that is alone: for [if] he falleth, there is not a second to lift him up. (Eccl 4:8–10)

Anyone who works knows that things do not always turn out as anticipated. In practical affairs, unexpected challenges appear, mistakes are made, and external circumstances interfere with the smooth progression of the process. To expect that things will always run smoothly and produce a perfect product every time is to harbor delusions. The wise are those who know how to keep their expectations within reasonable limits, to take steps to recognize and inhibit potential threats, and to accept gracefully whatever contradictions or reversals come their way. The myth of continual progress is not only unsound; ultimately it is also disheartening.

Diminishment

Qoheleth recognized that there is virtue in accepting to be average. Statistically, that is what most of us are, and recognizing this is a great step forward. The much-flaunted "pursuit of excellence" is often no more than a feeble attempt to disguise mediocrity by seeking distinction in one narrow avenue of achievement. Those who are considered to be highly endowed in one area usually counterbalance this by being underendowed in another. A champion boxer may well lack the skills to become a micro-surgeon. The impractical and absent-minded professor is a comic trope in many cultures. This leads to the conclusion that we ourselves and the lives we have fashioned for ourselves are also (subjectively) mixtures of positive and negative components. This approach accords with the concise statement of Job: "If we accept good from God, we must also accept evil" (Job 2:10). We can kick against the goad all we like, we can blame others, we can curse our bad luck, but mixity is a universal characteristic of human life. Qoheleth's duality is not cosmological, like that of the Persians; it is psychological and moral. The precise blend of desirable and undesirable elements within us is due to choices that we have made. We have the capacity to make things worse for ourselves. To the extent that we have allowed ourselves to become attached to vanities then, progressively, our whole being becomes more radically divided between reality and non-reality with an emerging preference for what is delusional.

In the vicissitudes of a normal life much depends on the subjective value we attribute to particular possibilities. If good health is a priority, illness is seen as a disaster. If there is a craving for material resources beyond everything else, penury makes life unlivable. If we unrealistically desire wisdom or virtue, then our single-minded pursuit of such laudable goals—despite their being beyond the reach of most of us—can blight our everyday existence as much as embracing total depravity. In truth, no one is exempt from the inclination to sin. It is useless to try to deny it. "This is evil among all that is done under the sun, that there is one condition to all, and also the heart of the sons of men is full of evil, and madness is in their hearts while they live, and after that, they go to the dead" (Eccl 9:3). Trying to be what we cannot be is the ultimate folly; accepting life within our natural limits is a good foundation for practical wisdom. And it can be a point of departure to extending those limits:

> Be not thou just overmuch, neither make thyself over-
> wise: wherefore shouldest thou be desolate? Be not

thou wicked overmuch, neither be thou foolish: wherefore shouldest thou perish not in thy time? It is good that thou lay hold on this: but yet withdraw not thine hand from that: for he that feareth God shall come forth of them all. (Eccl 7:16–18)

In the context of the mixity of created things, we ought to strive to accept with good grace all life's contrarieties; to wish to eliminate what does not immediately please us is, ultimately, to impoverish our lives. There is a providence, surely, even in our failures to meet our self-imposed standards. "Surely there is no man [who is] just on the earth, that doeth good and sinneth not" (Eccl 7:20). Furthermore, the demand that we make of ourselves that we understand everything is unreasonable. This is the paradox, that "[God] hath set the world in their heart, yet man cannot find out the work that God hath wrought from the beginning even to the end" (Eccl 3:11). What we as humans desire is beyond the scope of our minds and wills to encompass. If we are wise, we learn to accommodate this ambiguity. Desire is an energizing force within us, but only if it remains unsatisfied. When desire is fulfilled, it disappears. So it is good for us that we want more than we can possibly attain.

It was the prevailing presupposition of Hebrew wisdom that a long life was an unequivocal benefit. Typical is the text in the Book of Proverbs: "My son, do not forget my teaching but keep my commandments in your heart, for they will bring you long life, many years and great prosperity" (Prov 3:1–2). But, just as for every bright light there is an equally dark shadow, so apparent benefits often have hidden liabilities. Qoheleth is acutely aware that as the years pile up, so do bodily infirmities. Bodies wear out. Senescence brings with it a diminution in our faculties; at its worst, it becomes senility. In a cautionary admonition to the young, the Preacher tells them to enjoy their youthful vigor while it lasts, because it will not endure indefinitely:

> Though a man live many years, and in them all he rejoice, yet he shall remember the days of darkness, because they are many, all that cometh is vanity.
>
> Rejoice, O young man, in thy youth, and let thine heart cheer thee in the days of thy youth: and walk in the ways of thine heart, and in the sight of thine eyes: but know that for all these things, God will bring thee to judgment. Therefore take away grief out of thine heart, and cause evil to depart from thy flesh: for childhood and youth are vanity. (Eccl 11:8–10)

The text continues with an evocation of the multiple diminishments experienced as life draws to a close:

> Remember now thy Creator in the days of thy youth, whilst the evil days come not, nor the years approach, wherein thou shalt say, I have no pleasure in them: Whilst the sun is not dark, nor the light, nor the moon, nor the stars, nor the clouds return after the rain: When the keepers of the house shall tremble, and the strong men shall bow themselves, and the grinders shall cease, because they are few, and they wax dark that look out by the windows: And the doors shall be shut without by the base sound of the grinding, and he shall rise up at the voice of the bird: and all the daughters of singing shall be abased. Also they shall be afraid of the high thing, and fear shall be in the way, and the almond tree shall flourish, and the grasshopper shall be a burden, and concupiscence shall be driven away: for man goeth to the house of his age, and the mourners go about in the street. Whilst the silver cord is not lengthened, nor

the golden ewer broken, nor the pitcher broken at the well, nor the wheel broken at the cistern. And dust returns to the earth as it was, and the spirit returns to God that gave it. (Eccl 12:1–7)

This important and poetic passage offers us a key to understanding Qoheleth's basic philosophy of life. He begins by noting that, even in a predominantly happy existence, there are many dark days. The shadow of *hevel* hangs over everything. Youth is an era of absolutes. As the years increase, so does a sense that every aspect of human experience has only relative value; everything is contingent, impermanent, and ambiguous. But this realization does not make moments of exhilaration less desirable. On the contrary, they are to be more ardently embraced because they are acknowledged as fleeting. As only an older man can, the Preacher recognizes the many advantages with which God has gifted youth. Enthusiasm, passion, optimism, energy, resilience, and certainty: all are precious endowments and it is through their agency that good things happen, and the world is made a better place. Qoheleth encourages the young to follow these natural inclinations, to "walk in the ways of thine heart, and in the sight of thine eyes" (Eccl 11:9). They are not to become prematurely old and wise, but to be as they are: young and, perhaps, a little foolish. To be themselves and, at the same time, recognize that they are responsible for their actions and that, at some point, they may have to answer for their choices. As they grow older, they may find that, from time to time, they have to reverse course. And there will be a moment for judgment which will determine the price to be paid for past errors. This prospect, however, should not prevent their enjoying their youth while it lasts—because it will not continue indefinitely.

Qoheleth moves on to remind them of the diminishment they will experience when old age comes upon them. The effects of senescence are described by an impressionistic and cinematic *tour d'horizon*. The camera pans around the various sights and sounds and events that constitute everyday life and records their diminished impact. It is not a systematic listing of symptoms but a signaling of the disintegration and diminution of ordinary life experiences. But meanwhile, everything around us follows its normal routines, regardless of our drifting away from it. There is pathos here. The brashness of youthful exuberance has given way to an enfeebled response to the world and its doings. All the elements that hitherto constituted the substance of daily experience have ceased to have much of an impact. They are broken and left desolate. Excitement and *joie de vivre* are things of the past.[6]

---

6. I see no necessity for reading the elements of this poetic evocation of age as a systematic listing of specific ailments. Saint Jerome's attempts to do so appear somewhat crass to me: *Commentarius in Ecclesiasten, Patrologia Latina* 23, 1164. He is followed in this line of interpretation by Alcuin, *Commentaria super Ecclesiasten, Patrologia Latina* 100, 716–718; and also by the *Glossa Ordinaria*. Jennifer Lynn Kostoff Käärd, "The 'Glossa Ordinaria' on Ecclesiastes: A Critical Edition with Introduction" (doctoral dissertation, University of Toronto, 2015), 293–95. In a riff on this passage, which he interprets as a series of metaphors, Rabbi Rami Shapiro paints the following picture of old age: "Your eyes grow cloudy with cataracts…. [There are problems with] your teeth. Your eyes. You cannot move your bowels. Your digestion is poor. You cannot sleep through the night for all the noise, yet you cannot hear people speaking to you during the day. Your balance is wobbly, and you fear stumbling over any uneven surface. Your nerves are so sensitive that almost anything causes irritation. Your spinal column loses all flexibility, and your back is in spasm. You fall and crack your skull. You suffer from vomiting and acid reflux. You become incontinent." Shapiro, *Ecclesiastes: Annotated and Explained* (Woodstock, VT: SkyLight Paths, 2010), 104–6. Roland Murphy remarks that "the application of the physiological allegory shows a certain arbitrariness. There is simply no agreement on specifics." Roland Murphy, *Ecclesiastes* (Dallas: Word Books, 1992), 118.

But here is a qualification to be noted. In the light of what Qoheleth has written elsewhere in the book, the diminishment that comes with aging must also have positive aspects. This is part of God's creative plan for humanity—a plan that can only serve to our advantage. Even while we find ourselves forced to withdraw from the helter-skelter of busy interaction with our surroundings, we also are progressively insulated from its irritants and annoyances. We don't get upset as often as we used to. We are less bothered by the idiocies surrounding us. There can be a charm and serenity in old age that was absent in the years of active involvement with issues and projects. This mellowness is the obverse of what is perceived as diminishment when the body wears out and slows down. Just as there is a shadow side to every bright moment, so old age is not all gloom; it has its own subtle benedictions.

Nevertheless, it has to be admitted that the disparate manifestations of declining liveliness are harbingers of that final moment of separation when the person parts company with the world, and the physical organism which had hitherto sustained the contact enters into dissolution. Old age makes the thought of death ever more intrusive, especially as more of our contemporaries precede us into the shadowland beyond.

Death

In an earlier chapter, we spoke of the remembrance of our death as a significant component of wisdom. Death is the ultimate and definitive diminishment. All is lost. Just as there is a time to be born, there will be a time in which we die (cf. Eccl 3:2), but when this will be is not known to us (cf. Eccl 6:6). Death is the ineluctable fate of every human being, just as it is with the animals (cf. Eccl 3:18–21). All that has been gained in a lifetime of endeavor slips away from one's grasp. One's material possessions pass to heirs, be they worthy or not. One's preferences and priorities need no longer be taken into consideration. If one's passing leaves a gap, it is soon filled in—without reference to one's wishes. The world continues as if one had never existed.

> As he came forth of his mother's belly, he shall return naked to go as he came, and shall bear away nothing of his labor, which he hath caused to pass by his hand. And this also is an evil sickness that in all points as he came, so shall he go, and what profit hath he that he hath travailed for the wind? (Eccl 5:14–15)

It is death which reveals the utter vanity (*hevel*) of life. If one as richly endowed as King Solomon (cf. Eccl 2:3–11) had evaded death, he would truly have been omnipotent. But, subject as he was to the universal law of death, his ultimate fate is no different from ours. He has no more direct impact on everyday life than we will have. He is dead. As Qoheleth memorably remarks, a living dog is much better off than a dead lion (cf. Eccl 9:4–6). Everything that seems to be a benefit in this life has only transitory value; our claim to it ceases when we die.

We do not know what happens to dead human beings. Although their visible activity ceases, yet maybe a certain passivity remains. We will not be able to do anything, and we will be totally powerless to resist anything that might be done to us. Just as we have no direct control over what will happen to our corpse, so the fate of whatever else is left of us does not remain in our own hands. Qoheleth seems convinced that after death all of us will be subject to judgment (cf. Eccl 11:9). Yet the shape of this assessment is hidden from us. For the time being, the punishment of sin and the reward of virtue are delayed, so we cannot judge the moral status of a person by their current situation. The case of Job is a verification of this principle.

After death, however, things will be different. Then there will be a judgment:

> Because sentence against an evil work is not executed speedily, therefore the heart of the children of men is fully set in them to do evil. Though a sinner do evil a hundred times, and God prolongeth his days, yet I know that it shall be well with them that fear the Lord, and do reverence before him. But it shall not be well to the wicked, neither shall he prolong his days: he shall be like a shadow, because he feareth not before God. (Eccl 8:11–13)

While professing ignorance about what happens after death (cf. Eccl 12:7), the Preacher seems relatively certain that God will, in some manner, intervene to redress the imbalances of this present life. The spirit will rise to God and there will be a judgment. And the Epilogist adds, "For God will bring every work unto judgment, with every secret thing, whether it be good or evil" (Eccl 12:14). And after the judgment we go to our eternal home (cf. Eccl 12:5). It seems that, according to Qoheleth, though we have lost everything in death, something of us will still remain.

In the matter of death, as with everything else important in human existence, we are made powerfully aware of the limits of our knowledge. We do not know what happens at death, nor can we imagine what occurs afterwards. Thus, the idea of death can serve as a reminder of how little we understand about ourselves and about the world in which we live and how likely it is that many of the things about which we make such a fuss are no more substantial than a dying breath. Indeed, all is *hevel*.

6

GOOD TIMES

In a world characterized by continual change, the good news is that hardship cannot be unending. Everything is subject to alternation; nothing in this life lasts forever. When the clouds gather and all seems dark, we can be sure that a change will come—eventually. Yet, hard times seem to occupy more space in our memory and conversation. Happy days are self-legitimating; we accept them at their face value and enjoy them. And if they do not completely slip out of our memory, they merge into a generalized feeling of well-being. Negative experiences, however, are easily remembered in every painful detail; they continue in the present to generate feelings of anger and resentment that are sometimes even stronger than what we felt originally. It has been remarked of certain famous writers that they are more eloquent when declaiming their dissatisfaction and disgust than when they write about something that brought them pleasure. The same is true of the Book of Psalms; even though its Hebrew title is *sefer tehillim* (the book of praises), the largest category of psalms is that of laments. Our troubles have a disproportionate influence on our general attitude to life.

It is worth remembering that in Ecclesiastes, despite first impressions, the word "good" occurs more often than "evil"

(51 times compared with 30 [*r'h*] + 12 [*rs'*]), and "wise" more than "foolish" (51 times compared with 18 [*ksyl*] + 13 [*skl*] + 7 [*hll*]). Notwithstanding the frequency of terms for "vanity," "toil," "trouble," and "vexation," there are seventeen strong references to *simchah*, "joy," "enjoyment," or "pleasure." It has been suggested that for Qoheleth, "'enjoyment' not 'work' is to be our controlling metaphor of life."[1] Whatever diminishes joy diminishes life. Without joy, we are as good as dead.

The texts that speak strongly of this theme recur throughout the book:

> Therefore I see that there is nothing better than that a man should rejoice in his affairs, because that is his portion. For who shall bring him to see what shall be after him? (Eccl 3:22)

The Preacher suggests that we should find enjoyment in whatever task we are engaged. This is, clearly, a key to a happy life. The obvious conclusion is that the level of enjoyment experienced in a particular work depends more on the subjective disposition of the worker than on the particular character of the work. Unlike the prodigal son, I have never cleaned out a pigsty, but I imagine that, if one were rightly disposed, one could experience some level of delight in the task, noting its progress with satisfaction and being proud and pleased with its final state. At the very least, I would be glad to see the job finished. However, I can also imagine one engaged in the same task grumbling and feeling victimized, taking no care with the work and ending up more disgruntled than at the beginning. It may seem simple-minded, but there is wisdom in just giving

---

1. Robert K. Johnston, "'Confessions of a Workaholic': A Reappraisal of Qoheleth," *Catholic Biblical Quarterly* 38, no. 1 (January 1976), 18.

oneself fully to whatever has to be done, without rebellion or recrimination. Notice the clause "for that is his portion (*cheleq*)." It calls for an acceptance that the assignment of this task is due ultimately to the providence of God. This means that giving oneself wholly to its completion is an act of faith and obedience to God. Any task activates an otherwise latent faith when it is accepted that this task is part of God's benevolent plan—although we cannot ascertain its ultimate purpose or direction. This means that we have to impose a moratorium on our tendency to evaluate every possibility that confronts us according to our own plans and purposes. Otherwise, we may end up rejecting a course of action that would be ultimately beneficial to ourselves and, maybe, to the world. Qoheleth often emphasizes that we do not perceive the whole picture, and so, we are not in a position to make precipitate judgments on the value of anything. If we are wise, we recognize our limits. We try to avoid racing to deliver a judgment.

As we shall discuss in the next chapter, Qoheleth has a consistent preference for the present over the future. Making the most of each day, such as it is, is more important than placing all one's hope in a future that is far from certain—and it is best to strike while the iron is hot. Who knows whether present possibilities will remain open tomorrow? The Preacher advises:

> Also to every man to whom God hath given riches and treasures, and giveth him power to eat thereof, and to take his [portion], and to enjoy his labor: this is the gift of God. Surely he will not much remember the days of his life, because God answereth to the joy of his heart. (Eccl 5:18–19)

All the elements of our life come gratuitously from the hand of God. The gifts we have been given, whether they include material resources or other benefits, are for our enjoyment and, perhaps, meant as a contribution to our common welfare. The portion we have been assigned, including our toil ('amal), is intended as a source of happiness. Again, we notice the whimsical injunction to enjoy even our toil. This unshakeable will for happiness means that we will not waste our moments in brooding over the negativities of the past or the inconveniences—or worse—of the present.

The final clause has been the object of much discussion: "because God answereth to the joy of his heart." The more usual translation is: "God keeps [him] busy with the joy of his heart." This reading is supported by both the Septuagint Greek and the Vulgate Latin. The sense would seem to be that when all goes well and we are happy, we do not dwell on the past or fear the future. Norbert Lohfink, however, has proposed that the clause is to be understood in the sense that the self-revelation of God occurs through the heart's joy. Everyday happiness is meant to give us a taste for the spiritual world. "The joy of the heart must be something like divine revelation."[2] God is the source of our joy. The encounter with God results in an experience of deep happiness for the human being, a happiness which surpasses any of the many sources of happiness to be found in the world around us. This transcendent joy generates a forgetfulness of everyday life and causes us to look beyond this world of space and time for the ultimate meaning of life. It is a call to "follow the ecstasy." Every moment of joy is like an invitation to redefine ourselves not by the negativities we have endured but also by the precious experience of bliss that comes to us from time to time:

---

2. Norbert Lohfink, "Qoheleth 5:17–19—Revelation by Joy," *Catholic Biblical Quarterly* 32, no. 4 (October 1990), 634. The argument is rather technical; it centers on the different roots of 'nh distinguished in dictionaries.

> And I praised joy: for there is no goodness to man under the sun, save to eat and to drink and to rejoice: for this is adjoined to his labor, the days of his life that God hath given him under the sun. (Eccl 8:15)

The Preacher praises joy as a necessary component of goodness. Our willingness to experience joy should be untinged by any feelings of guilt or regret. The receptivity of the joy that leads us to God begins with our openness to enjoy God's everyday gifts, in particular, food and drink. It is a spurious spirituality which recommends that we completely forgo the pleasurable satisfaction of simple natural needs in favor of loftier ambitions. Temperance is a virtue that is identified with moderation. Virtue stands in a middle place, avoiding both too much and too little. Denial of our appetites is dangerous. We need to negotiate with our instinctual needs to find a compromise that recognizes their validity and, at the same time, is truly life-giving for us. Saint Paul's advice in particular instances illustrates this principle. He advises married couples: "Do not deprive one another except perhaps by agreement for a set time, to devote yourselves to prayer, and then come together again, so that Satan may not tempt you because of your lack of self-control" (1 Cor 7:5). And Timothy is advised not to be too abstinent: "Take a little wine for your stomach's sake" (1 Tim 5:23). Sometimes, a strategic withdrawal from unrealizable and noble ideals is necessary to ensure that they do not become unintentionally destructive. At least, this is what Saint Jerome seemed to believe:

> The human mind is not able always to stretch out to the sublime and to think about divine and loftier matters, nor is it able to be permanently in contemplation of heavenly realities. Sometimes it must defer to bodily necessities. There is a time for embracing wisdom

and for clinging to it more closely, and a time for relaxing the mind from the gaze and embrace of wisdom so that it might be of service to the care of the body and to those things that are needed for our life—apart from sin.[3]

There are many who unconsciously equate pleasure with sin, so that alongside every silver lining there is a gray cloud of guilt to cover it. Perhaps we might take comfort in the teaching of Saint Thomas Aquinas that pleasure or delight (*delectatio*) in itself is simply an indication that something is in accordance with nature and, therefore, good and virtuous. He writes that "no one is able to live without some sensual and bodily delight" and "because delight is a quietening of an appetite in something good, if that in which the appetite finds quiet is simply good then there will simply be delight and that will be simply good."[4] Enjoyment of what is intrinsically enjoyable, such as eating and drinking, is an indication of harmony with nature, whereas a failure to find pleasure in such activities indicates a disorder of some kind—bodily or psychological. Pope Paul VI reminded pastors that "there is also needed a patient effort to teach people, or teach them once

---

3. Saint Jerome, *Commentarius in Ecclesiasten, Patrologia Latina* 23, 1089C. See also the *Glossa Ordinaria* on Eccl 3:5: *Et propter copoream necessitatem, tempus est relaxandi mentem a complexu sapientiae, ut curae corporis serviatur.* "Because of bodily necessity, there is a time for relaxing the mind from the embrace of wisdom, so that care of the body may be maintained." Jennifer Lynn Kostoff Käärd, "The 'Glossa Ordinaria' on Ecclesiastes: A Critical Edition with Introduction" (doctoral dissertation, University of Toronto, 2015), 206.

4. Thomas Aquinas, *Summa Theologiae* 1-II, 34.1; and 1-II, 34.2. In his discussion of temperance in *ST* 2-II, 168, he defends play as being a necessary lubricant of human interaction and also observes that mirth is useful for the relaxation and pleasure it brings.

more, how to savor in a simple way the many human joys that the Creator places in our path."[5]

Saint Bernard of Clairvaux goes further, seeing our bodily life as a necessary first stage in the life to which we shall enter after death. The flesh—even with all its pomps and works—is to be cherished. "I do not say that you should hate your own flesh. Love it as something given to you as a helper, and made ready to be your partner in eternal happiness."[6] Spirituality is often tempted to a dualistic attitude to the body, seeing it at best as inferior, at worst as hostile. Qoheleth's robust approach to life helps us to withstand this temptation:

> Go, eat thy bread with joy, and drink thy wine with a cheerful heart: for God now accepteth thy works. At all times let thy garments be white, and let not oil be lacking upon thine head. Rejoice with the wife whom thou hast loved all the days of the life of thy vanity, which God hath given thee under the sun all the days of thy vanity: for this is thy portion in the life, and in thy travail wherein thou laborest under the sun. All that thine hand shall find to do, do it with all thy power: for there is neither work nor invention, nor knowledge, nor wisdom in the grave whither thou goest. (Eccl 9:7–10)

Commentators remark that the Hebrew notion of joy (*simchah*) is not merely an interior experience. Rejoicing goes as deep as the heart (Eccl 5:19), but finds external manifestation in ways that are sometimes boisterous. "Joy expresses itself in

---

5. Pope Paul VI, *Gaudete in Domino*, Apostolic Exhortation on Christian Joy (May 9, 1975).

6. Bernard of Clairvaux, *Sermons on Psalm 90* 10.3; *Sancti Bernardi Opera* (Rome: Editiones Cistercienses, 1957–1978), 4:444.

frisking about (Jer 50:11), clapping (Ezek 25:6), dancing, shouting, and singing."[7] Psalm 150 speaks of dancing with trumpets, lutes, harps, tambourines, strings, pipes, and cymbals. This is more than a deep interior serenity, it is a boisterous, bodily celebration. In such a context, it is not surprising that joy is understood as being generated by carnal activities like eating and drinking, working and loving. These are everyday activities accessible to almost everyone. There is, therefore, no reason for anyone not to live life in a celebratory mode, wearing splendid clothing and anointing oneself with oil to make the face shine. And since it is not good for a man to be alone, Qoheleth includes among the components of a joyful life the lifelong companionship of a beloved spouse. There is much in life that is frustrating and oppressive—everything is subject to the law of *hevel*—and so it is necessary to avail oneself wholeheartedly of whatever pleasures happen to come our way. These happy days are as much part of our portion as the negativities that cause us grief. The days of joy are also God's gifts to us.

Again, the Preacher urges us to enjoy our life and our work while we can, since our span on earth is limited and there is no guarantee that we will be able to make up for missed opportunities later on. The end of life is never far from his mind. It serves to heighten the urgency of his appeal that we do not let present possibilities of pleasure pass us by; they are necessarily counterbalances to the inevitable irritants of our common human life on earth. Without making the most of them, we will scarcely be able to cope. After every exertion, relaxation and recuperation are important steps toward recovery.

---

7. G. Vanoni, art. "*Samach* etc.," *Theological Dictionary of the Old Testament XIV* (Grand Rapids: Eerdmans, 2004), 149. See also Hennie Kruger, "Laughter in the Old Testament: A Hotchpotch of Humour, Mockery and Rejoicing?" *In die Skriflig* 48.2, Art #712, http://dx.doi.org/10.4102/ids.v4812.712.

Pleasure is an automatic response to stimulation. As such, it is not under the direct control of reason. Reason, guided by experience, can avoid or offset the sources of stimulation, but once the point of no return is passed, pleasure becomes autonomous. As such, pleasure is often assumed to be close to sinful, especially thanks to the efforts of those who hold the body in disdain: compulsive moralizers and philosophical dualists. And there have been ascetics who have lost sight of the ultimate goal of their spiritual endeavor and allowed themselves to find a perverse pleasure simply in avoiding all pleasure and even in self-inflicted pain. The Preacher, however, reminds us that the experience of pleasure is natural and a gift of God that, although it coexists with *hevel*, is not conquered by it.

Sometimes Qoheleth is charged with being an Epicurean, by which it is crudely suggested that he was advocating a kind of hedonism. Although the ideas of Epicurus were in circulation at the time Ecclesiastes was written, any direct influence is unlikely. Qoheleth's advocacy of enjoying what life offers must be interpreted as being entirely consistent with his observations concerning the impermanence and fragility of everything. Pleasure is an appropriate response to whatever is pleasurable; as such, it is virtuous. Nevertheless, Alcuin (725–804) ended his commentary on the book with a cautionary poem: "Let the young man peruse [this book] with great moderation of mind, lest he rush forward into the trap of Epicurus."[8] Far from becoming hedonists, most superficial readers are more likely to end up in the slough of despond.

Surely the light is a pleasant thing: and it is a good thing to the eyes to see the sun. Though a man live

---

8. *Quem tuus, o iuvenis! tanto moderamine sensus / Perlegat, Epicuri ne ruat in foveam.* Alcuin, *Commentaria super Ecclesasten,* in *Patrologia Latina* 100, 720.

many years, and in them all he rejoice, yet he shall remember the days of darkness, because they are
many, all that cometh is vanity. Rejoice, O young
man, in thy youth, and let thine heart cheer thee in
the days of thy youth: and walk in the ways of thine
heart, and in the sight of thine eyes: but know that for
all these things, God will bring thee to judgment.
Therefore take away grief out of thine heart, and
cause evil to depart from thy flesh: for childhood and
youth are vanity. (Eccl 11:7–10)

We are to enjoy life's pleasures, yet its contrariety remains.
Natural goodness is self-legitimating but it is not unlimited.
Light is to be enjoyed, but without becoming forgetful of the
encroaching darkness. Qoheleth speaks as an older man,
soberly mindful that troubles will come and that we will have
to take responsibility for the choices we have made. Even so,
we should not allow ourselves to be overwhelmed by the
prospect. If we are young, we should act our age and not attempt to be overwise or over-virtuous (Eccl 7:16). Everything
is transitory. Most of us gather a bit of wisdom as the years roll
by. We learn from our own mistakes and by observing the folly
of others. It is unfair to expect the young to have this experien-
tial knowledge; they will acquire it readily enough without
having to be taught. Meanwhile, it has been observed that "ge-
nius (and talent) are usually associated with youth. Wisdom
and competence are the fruits of maturity.... Wisdom and
competence are the rewards of aging."[9] There is complemen-
tarity here. There is value both in bold youthful exuberance
and in the calm, calibrated experience of the senior. The main

---

9. Elkhonon Goldberg, *The Wisdom Paradox: How Your Mind Can
Grow Stronger as Your Brain Grows Older* (New York: Gotham Books,
2005), 80.

priority is for each age to be true to itself and to respect those with different capabilities. Society needs to be sustained by both ends of the age spectrum.

Just as there is certainly a season for weeping, there is also a season for boisterous rejoicing (cf. Eccl 3:4). Such is life. Even though immoderate laughter is seen as the mark of a fool and we are admonished to prefer the house of mourning to the house of mirth (cf. Eccl 7:7), Qoheleth's plan for living includes a generous helping of happiness. We are to allow life's little pleasures to exercise their magic on us and to alleviate some of the heaviness we experience as a result of being immersed in *hevel*. This is not a case of blind eudemonism. The Preacher's philosophy does not fear to include in its purview all the "labors, pains, weariness, poverty, bereavement, all types of illness, and trouble" that constitute the lot of humankind. Indeed, he makes a point of emphasizing their universality. But he does not stop there. Somehow, joy has to discover a way to coexist with these existential pangs.

The Barriers to Joy

Joy is an unambiguous benefit. We all want to be happy. This assertion is not contradicted by the fact that some people seem to enjoy being miserable; it is simply a matter that they find perverse joy in inflicting their own gloom upon others. It seems to me that if we do not experience a predominance of joy in our life it is because we think of joy in terms of passivity. In such cases, we experience joy only when others do good for us or when our projects prosper or something nice crops up in our life. Such a perspective sees joy as the result of what happens outside us and merely impinges on us. Our subjective state is entirely dependent on realities outside ourselves. Inevitably, because we live in a changing universe, such an expectation often leads to disappointment, and sadness results. We then blame others for our negative moods. They did not do for us what we had anticipated, events did not turn out as we had hoped. What is happening is that we have abandoned responsibility for the quality of our lives and left them at the mercy of the interplay of extraneous factors. Instead, our lives should be marked by a preferential option for happiness: it becomes the criterion by which we judge alternative courses of action. Will it bring me happiness? Not just immediately but permanently.

One cause of the persistent malaise of misery is that we lack the virtue of creative self-doubt. Our personal opinions and preferences have become absolute. We no longer acknowledge that these are always conditioned by multiple influences in our past and present, and can quickly change when our circumstances are modified. And, moreover, we are reluctant to admit that there are limits to our knowledge and experience. For the moment, our preferences feel absolute; and if the universe does not render fealty to them, we become disgruntled. "I want what I want, and I want it now." We recognize this as a very infantile approach to life, yet all of us know adults for whom this seems to be a permanent stance in their everyday dealings. Happiness is a demand they make of others; they themselves are only its consumers. Perhaps the darkest words in our language are, "If only..." — if only this had not happened, if only I had obtained this, if only others had been kinder to me, if only things had turned out differently. The cause of our misery is thought to be outside ourselves — we fail to acknowledge our complicity in contributing to our own unhappiness both by what we do and by what we have failed to do.

Pondering on the words of the Preacher may well lead to a way out of this impasse, at least on a rational level. If everything is *hevel*, as Qoheleth avers, then nothing has the power to change the way things are. Things are as they are; we have to adapt to them, not vice versa. They will not change themselves to suit our preferences. In any case, once we are gone, our priorities will no longer matter to anyone. "Also their love, and their hatred, and their envy is now perished, and they have no more portion forever, in all that is done under the sun" (Eccl 9:6). Meanwhile we have only a limited arena in which we can effect even partial change. What is more important is that we begin to change ourselves. In other words, we begin to accept the proposition that we need to be adaptable to the changes that take place around us. This means, in the first place, that we stop regretfully dreaming that the past was a Golden Age and so being led to conclude that, because the good old days no longer exist, we are exempt from action: "Say not thou, 'Why is it that the former days were better than these?' for thou dost not enquire wisely of this thing" (Eccl 7:12). Equally, we are admonished not to mortgage the present in the hope of a better future: "For he knoweth not that which shall be: for who can tell him when it shall be?" (Eccl 8:7). And: "Man knoweth not what shall be: and who can tell him what shall be after him?" (Eccl 10:14). Nor is one able to foresee a sudden change in fortune, for "time and chance cometh to them all. For neither doth man know his time, but as the fishes which are taken in an evil net, and as the birds that are caught in the snare: so are the children of men snared in the evil time when it falleth upon them sudden" (Eccl 9:12).

Meanwhile the relentless cycle of life and death continues inexorably. There is only a limited amount that we can do to change its course:

> One generation passeth, and another generation succeedeth: but the earth remaineth forever. The sun riseth, and the sun goeth down, and draweth to his place, where he riseth. The wind goeth toward the

South, and compasseth toward the North: the wind goeth round about, and returneth by his circuits. All the rivers go into the sea, yet the sea is not full: for the rivers go unto the place whence they return and go. All things are full of labor: man cannot utter it: the eye is not satisfied with seeing, nor the ear filled with hearing. What is it that hath been [in the past], that shall be [in the present]: and what is done [in the present] shall be done [in the future]: and there is no new thing under the sun. Is there anything whereof one may say, Behold this, it is new? It hath been already in the old time that was before us. (Eccl 1:6–10)

To rebel against reality is the ultimate folly. If we cannot change things outside ourselves, then the only way to improve a situation which we judge to be unsatisfactory is to change ourselves. To modify the interface between ourselves and reality. To adopt an alternative stance in the face of things that are beyond our power to change. To see things differently and to craft a different response.

If there is always a glimmer of a doubt concerning our reading of the present situation, then there is some possibility that what now appears to be totally negative may yet yield some positive effects. I was late and I missed my flight, but the plane on which I was due to fly crashed; mysteriously my life was saved. I fell over in the street but was rescued by a stranger, and so began one of the strongest friendships in my life. Again and again, Qoheleth reminds us that we do not have the overarching knowledge that God has, and so we are liable to see less than the total picture; this causes us to arrive at defective judgments:

For who knoweth what is good for man in the life and in the number of the days of the life of his vanity, seeing he maketh them as a shadow? For who can show unto man what shall be after him under the sun? (Eccl 7:2)

Thou knowest not what evil shall be upon the earth. (Eccl 11:2)

Then I beheld the whole work of God, that man cannot find out the work that is wrought under the sun: for the which man laboreth to seek it, and cannot find it: yea, and though the wise man think to know it, he cannot find it. (Eccl 8:17)

A realistic philosophy of life recognizes the limits that we experience in the world around us and in ourselves, and seeks to accommodate itself to them. It embraces a strategy of being non-reactive, of not allowing itself to be automatically determined by external events or the antics of others. Rather than protesting and seeking to change them, the philosophic mind simply recalibrates its response in order to minimize harm and, where possible, to navigate toward a positive outcome. Kicking against the goad yields nothing but a sore toe. Accurately assessing the possibilities of the present and exploiting them for the purpose of achieving a better outcome serve much better than infantile tantrums. According to the common saying, it is better to light a candle than to curse the darkness.

There are four tendencies we find first in others—and only faintly and eventually in ourselves—which prevent people from taking reality seriously. It is as though we consider that which is not to be usually preferable to that which is—a perverse form of the Hindu practice of *Neti...Neti* (not this, not that). Nothing is able to satisfy them. Such people often refuse to be happy until everything conforms to their wishes. By identifying these symptoms in others, we may begin to move toward the recognition of their presence within ourselves and so have the opportunity to do something to remedy the situation.

Control.
Those with a compulsive need to be in control of every situation in which they find themselves are drawn into an ongoing conflict with reality. Because they cannot accept that there are elements in the universe that will not submit to their wise direction, they are in a constant state of dudgeon, unable to attain any depth of unqualified happiness. They attempt to impose their will on their immediate situation, on their relationships, and—if they could—even on the weather. When their efforts fail, they are glum. In an effort to assuage their existential insecurity, they seek to tame the wildness of reality with a plethora of rules, regulations, timetables, flowcharts, and hierarchies, so that nothing unanticipated may dare to poke its head above the placid surface of routine. If it does, there will be trouble. Fortunately for the rest of us, reality always defeats them. This means, however, that they are habitually unhappy and, often enough, generously share their unhappiness with those around them.

Perfectionism.
Another way of denying the reality of the world around us is to cultivate an attitude of perfectionism. Guided and goaded by an internalized parental voice, those afflicted with this malaise have a sharp eye for anything that is not exactly as it should be. Forgetting that perfection belongs to God alone, they hope to find it closer to home. It is not only those around them that are subjected to their idealistic standards; they also torture themselves by submitting their lives to lofty goals which transcend realistic attainment. They hate perceived failures or deficiencies with a self-punishing intensity. They have

no appreciation of the Japanese notion of the beauty of imperfection (*wabi-sabi*), which implies that the world is transient and impermanent—exactly as Qoheleth proclaims—but is still capable of moving the soul to admiration. Their extravagant expectations make their lives a misery that is not at all diminished by their compulsive efforts to render complete that which of its nature is necessarily incomplete.

Exceptionalism.
An exceptionalist tendency makes us believe that the ordinary conditions of human life on earth must somehow be modified to our advantage. We can bend the rules; they apply only to others. This is especially so in late adolescence where the connection is weak between the part of the brain that responds to instinctual prompting and that which assesses long-term consequences. Exceptionalists are always resentful and chafing at the bit, unwilling to accept that normal parameters apply also to them. Even though they claim special privileges for themselves, these seem not to assuage their desire for more. In fact, one may be led to suspect that the material advantages thus procured serve a mainly symbolic role—perhaps as surrogates for a loving acceptance that has not been experienced, especially in the early years.

Entitlement.
And yet, children reared by doting parents often grow up spoiled, with an especially keen sense of entitlement. Those with a strong sense of entitlement are often reluctant to share common resources. Once adulthood is attained, they expect to continue receiving the lavish level of attention and provision to which they have become accustomed. When this does not happen, they become permanently aggrieved. This provides them with a pretext to undervalue any expectation or obligation that others impose on them. They are unable to appreciate the

necessary conjunction of rights and duties. Rights they understand; duties habitually are beneath their radar. And they wonder why no social grouping can offer them the complete satisfaction they deserve, whether it be work, membership in a group, or marriage. There is little stability in their interaction because the give-and-take that this requires lacks one of its elements.

These causes of unhappiness, a tendency to control, perfectionism, exceptionalism, and an inflated sense of entitlement, are parts of what may be termed "individualism," the refusal to live in the context of others. Individualists live as though they do not accept the truth that "no man is an island." Human beings are societal animals; the best results accrue when they work together. Individualism is a crime against familial, tribal, national, and global solidarity. That it makes miserable the lives it touches is only to be expected. As the Preacher notes:

> Two are better than one: for they have better wages for their labor. For if they fall, the one will lift up his fellow: but woe unto him that is alone: for [if] he falleth, there is not a second to lift him up. Also if two sleep together, then shall they have heat: but to one how should there be heat? And if one overcome him, two shall stand against him: and a threefold cord is not easily broken. (Eccl 4:9–11)

To live in solidarity with others, respecting their different perspectives and granting leeway for their divergent desires, leads us to relativize our own perceptions and assessments. This creative self-doubt protects us from rash and often self-destructive impetuosity. We learn to step back and to judge things from an alternative standpoint. As a result, we are happier because we tend to make fewer mistakes. Furthermore, the fact of our having shown respect for others makes them happier and this joy also reverberates in us.

To many rapid readers, Qoheleth's moral prescriptions seem like a recipe for a fairly austere life. This is only partly true. By systematically undermining a false sense of happiness, the Preacher clears the way for a simple approach to living that is not overly upset by inevitable misfortunes and reversals and, at the same time, enthusiastically embraces all the little pleasures in which daily life abounds.

It is because *simchah* comes under the universal hegemony of *hevel*, and so is transitory and precarious, that we are urged to enjoy whatever moments of happiness that life affords us. We are not to allow the griefs of the past or our fears for the future to diminish our delight. The opportunity will not last indefinitely. The only time we have is now; we have to make the most of it.

7

CARPE DIEM

In one of his poems, the Roman poet Horace admonishes Leuconoë, his lady friend, not to seek to uncover the future from soothsayers, but to live in the present. "And cut long hope from this short span for, even as we speak, spiteful time flies away. Gather the day, for you cannot trust there will be another."[1]

From its starring role in the film *Dead Poets Society*, the phrase *Carpe diem* has often been translated as "Seize the day." The metaphor, however, is better understood in the context of gardening. *Carpe* is related to the Greek *arpázo karpon*, "to gather fruit." The sense of the admonition is, "Make haste to pick the fruit now; tomorrow is uncertain." A similar sentiment is found in Robert Herrick's 1648 poem "To the Virgins: to Make Much of Time":

Gather ye rosebuds while ye may,
Old Time is still a-flying;

---

1. ...*et spatio brevi / spem longam reseces, dum loquimur, fugerit invida / aetas: carpe diem, quam minimum credula postero. Odes* 1, 11; *The Odes of Horace*, ed. James Michie (Harmondsworth: Penguin, 1964), 38.

And this same flower that smiles today
Tomorrow will be dying.[2]

In both poems, there is a sense of urgency occasioned by the fact that the benefit that is possible today may not be possible tomorrow. We can have no certainty about what is to happen next. This is especially true when we attempt to predict the course of another person's life. Saint Augustine was keenly aware of this:

> What human can make a judgment about [another] human? Everything is filled with imprudent judgments. The one about whom we despaired is converted and becomes very good. The one whom we believed would do well suddenly fails and becomes very bad. Our fear is not certain nor is our love certain. A human being scarcely knows what [another] human being is today; and even if something is known about today, nothing is known about tomorrow.[3]

This is close to the heart of Qoheleth's message. The Preacher admonishes us to be present to the present while it is still present. It will not last. It is transitory. Soon this moment will be out of our reach. Our task is to inhabit each moment of time as it presents itself to us. To be fully present, with no seepage of attention to other times and other places. To live fully each moment is challenge enough. "One day, is that not enough for you?"[4] Because everything is fleeting, we must afford it our

---

2. *The Poems of Robert Herrick*, ed. L. C. Martin (London: Oxford University Press, 1965), 84.

3. Augustine of Hippo, *Sermo 46*, 27; *Corpus Christianorum Series Latina 41*, 553.

4. Pozzo in Samuel Beckett's, *Waiting for Godot: A Tragicomedy in Two Acts* (London: Faber and Faber, 1965), Act II, 89.

undivided attention. If important visitors arrived, most of us would drop everything to attend to them. Sadly, so many moments of our life pass us by unnoticed, as if unworthy of our attention. We might as well be dead, since "inattention is the death of the soul."[5]

Mindfulness

As animals with capacious brains, we have the possibility not only of attending to what stimulates our senses at a particular moment but also of carrying forward what happened to us in the past and projecting onto the present what might happen in the future. Such additions make for an enriched experience. However, this broader perspective often results in our giving only conditional acceptance to the present moment. Its voice is sometimes fainter than the voices that come from other times. Even the most intense experience can be modified by whispers from the past or the future, which give to this moment a different nuance or color. It sometimes seems that everything reminds us of something else—especially as the sum of our years increases.

Multi-faceted consciousness can be useful and enjoyable but, if left untrammeled, it can lead to kaleidoscopic confusion. This means that, if we are to extract everything that the present moment englobes, we have to make a concerted effort—to concentrate, to focus on the central experience to the exclusion of what lies at the periphery. We have all experienced how difficult it is to give all our attention to a delicate task when chaos breaks out around us. Parents working from home during the

---

5. *Mors animae oblivio.* Bernard of Clairvaux, *Sententiae* 2, 19; *Sancti Bernardi Opera* (Rome: Editiones Cistercienses, 1957–1978), 6b: 29.

pandemic found their efforts to concentrate undermined by the antics of their children. What we have learned from this is that when we need total application, we have to create a bubble for ourselves in which we can work without distraction. There is a lesson to be learned here; sometimes it is good to reduce our total sensory experience in order to go deeper. Less becomes more.

Ekagra (one-pointed) is a Sanskrit word which evokes the kind of preparation necessary for meditation. It involves slowly preventing the mind's lighthouse beam from its usual circular movement and causing it to shine only in a single direction. Once this relatively easy goal has been attained, a second reduction is necessary. The broad beam has to become a laser. This narrower shaft of light has the capacity to penetrate beneath what may be the meaningless external elements of the present moment to touch a deeper reality. The world of space and time becomes transparent. If it is true that eternity hides within the present,[6] then this concentration on the here and now has the capacity to bring us far beyond the experience of *hevel*—not by negating it, but by passing through it to the ultimate significance it has hitherto concealed from us. The "vanity" of all around us can be viewed as an indicator for us to keep moving, to pass on, and to reach out for that unknown reality beyond what we can experience in the here and now. Not that we can live constantly at this level. Such a profound experience occurs only sometimes,[7] but when it does happen it serves as a reminder that there is more to reality than immediately meets the eye.

The road that leads to such experiences—for they cannot be sought or procured directly—is the endeavor to live in a

---

6. *In momentaneo hoc latet aeternitas*. Bernard of Clairvaux, *Sermons on Psalm 90* 17.3; *Sancti Bernardi Opera* 4:488.

7. According to a medieval axiom, *rara hora et parva mora*: such experience is infrequent and of short duration.

state of emergent mindfulness. It is not a journey that can be accomplished in a couple of leaps and bounds. It is more likely to happen if one is fortunate enough to live a long life—it is a collateral benefit that serves as a counterweight to diminishing sensual and physical engagement. Constantly making the effort to live, attuned to reality, gives us occasional access to its whispered secrets.

Such a semi-habitual state is the result of multiple choices made in the course of a lifetime. It is the result of a happy harmony between the intellect and the will. Its early stages are marked by a progressive and systematic reduction in self-alienating activities. Our need to be entertained must be kept within appropriate limits. The state of having a double soul (*dipsuchia*) constantly pulled in opposite directions needs to give way to a certain simplicity or singleness of purpose, termed by the ancients "purity of heart."[8] They understood that, to arrive at this state, a person needs to embrace the practice of detachment or, as some prefer to call it, "non-attachment." To focus involves reducing the total area until it becomes a single point. This means letting go of much that was previously deemed to be both important and delightful, and concentrating on the one thing necessary.

The practice of mindfulness is costly because it involves progressive exclusion. In particular, concentration on the present moment involves a disciplined reduction in the influence that the past and the future exert on our experience of the here and now. Our reluctance to do this is mysterious. It sometimes seems that we do not want to be happy. We bring in elements from elsewhere that suck the joy out of the present moment. Instead of simply enjoying a cold beer on a hot

---

8. Søren Kierkegaard published a book with the title *Purity of Heart Is to Will One Thing: Spiritual Preparation for the Office of Confession*, trans. Douglas V. Steere (San Francisco: HarperOne, 2008).

summer's day, we allow ourselves to be bullied by the super-ego so that we fret about the drink's calorific count, its alcohol content, and the damage that might be done to our reputation if we are seen enjoying it. "Dead flies cause to stink, and pu-trefy the ointment of the apothecary" (Eccl 10:1). Today the weather is fine, but we fret because we do not know what to-morrow will be like. There sometimes seems to be a preferen-tial option for negative data, a suspicion of anything that seems to be good news.

Perhaps we need to find a counterweight to prevalent negativity by deliberately choosing to focus on what is good and pleasurable. As a beautiful aria by Handel advises: *Lascia la spina, cogli la rosa*, "Leave behind the thorns; gather the roses." This is not to deny that thorns exist and that precau-tions must be taken to avoid being hurt by them. It is, rather, a reasonable refusal to be defined by negativity or to revel in victimhood. Far from being a foolish optimism, it is simply the recognition that human life has both negative and positive features and that all is subject to the law of *hevel*. Neither good times nor bad times are permanent; all things are passing. At this moment, only the present is real. We can choose whether we focus on what is delightful or allow ourselves to be swamped by gloom.

There are collateral benefits to such a practice. For exam-ple, if we make the effort to be mindful of the food we are eat-ing, we will find that our pleasure is increased. If, instead of gulping down our food and then reaching for more, we allow ourselves to savor each mouthful and consciously appreciate the complex interplay of tastes and textures, we will find that eating becomes a more enjoyable experience. The psychologi-cal needs that, in addition to our physical hunger, prompt us to eat will be more fully assuaged, with the result that we will not be inclined to overeat. Believe it or not, really enjoying our food, mindful eating, is an important factor in any attempt at weight loss. Expanding this thesis, we could perhaps advance the suggestion that living more mindfully will prevent us from unknowingly falling into the clutches of any form of addictive behavior.

Mindfulness is not the same as total knowledge and comprehension. To accept reality often involves accepting its utter mystery. We do not always understand why particular things happen, no more than we understand why the universe exists. We can accept reality without understanding it. There is folly in rejecting anything that is beyond our capacity to understand. Quantum physics is not less true because I know nothing about it. Being mindful often involves suspending binary judgments about whether a situation or one of its elements is good or bad. If I offer you a glass of wine, you can either enjoy it or you can start making judgments. "I think Merlot is better than Shiraz; 1995 was not a good year for red wine; this glass is the wrong shape for this kind of wine...." If I knew what distress the wine would cause you, I would not have offered it! To the onlooker, identifying subjective preferences with objective qualities seems stupid, yet we do it all the time and, as a result, fail to wonder at the life-enhancing mysteries in which we are immersed. We are too busy concocting our petty assessments.

This relentless urge to constrict reality into categories that we can master leads to our living a diminished life. As Vladimir and Estragon agree in Beckett's *Waiting for Godot*: "To have lived is not enough for them. They have to talk about it...."[9] Life is meant to be lived; attempting to subject it to rational categories and discuss it is a distraction. Qoheleth would say that it is *hevel*. "For where there are many words there is much vanity" (Eccl 6:11). Wisdom is learning to accept reality in its totality, even when it cannot be fully explained,

---

9. Act II, 63.

and accordingly, one of the signs of maturing wisdom is being reluctant to offer snap judgments that are fueled more by opinion than by knowledge.

Obstacles to Mindfulness

To live mindfully is a noble aspiration, but not everyone who embraces this ideal remembers that mindfulness involves more than momentary concentration; it demands the systematic elimination of competing targets for our attention. Why do we fail to attend closely to our immediate circumstances or our immediate duties? The usual response is, "I was thinking of something else." Distractedness is a state with which we are all familiar. It takes many forms and owes its origins to many different causes, not all of them easily recognized. When our mind is wandering, we are unable to discern among available possibilities, and so fail to make the most of present opportunities. Our lives are poorer for our defective attention.

Here are eight overlapping factors that inhibit our capacity to take the present seriously and, therefore, to live mindfully.

Entertainment.
A first obstacle to living mindfully is our appetite for entertainment. Entertainment holds our attention and brings a measure of delight. It is a pleasurable diversion, allowing us for a while to leave the path we are treading and to find gratification elsewhere. Within reasonable limits, entertainment can bring solace to a heart wearied from daily struggles and rest to a mind that needs to withdraw from conscious application so as to recuperate and, eventually, to allow deeper thoughts to surface spontaneously. However, as the pursuit of entertainment becomes paramount, it begins to be an escape from reality and, inevitably, the quality of decision-making declines. Hours are

frittered away profitlessly, and progressively what takes place on the screen seems more real and more important than what is happening in our immediate neighborhood. Consequently, life becomes less meaningful. Playfulness is an important component of a complete human life, but it cannot be allowed to displace adult responsibility for the quality of one's life.

Fantasy.
When external entertainment is lacking, daydreaming can offer a partial remedy. Instead of being overwhelmed by the unyielding present, we betake ourselves somewhere else—usually to a place in our minds where needs that are not being met by reality are more than adequately fulfilled. If we experience failure, we fantasize about success; if we are lonely, we conjure up companionship; if we are timid, we transform ourselves into superheroes. Fantasy is the rejection of the present in favor of its diametric opposite. Often, it does relatively little harm, but if we overindulge in it, fantasy can squeeze reality out of our lives so that we end up in a state of emotional, or even mental, isolation from the real world. We begin to resent having to deal with reality when it intrudes, because it does not conform to the imaginary specifications we had attempted to impose on it. And we are less adept in dealing with it.

Compulsive Overwork and Multitasking.
Overwork is not due only to industriousness; it can also be an avoidance of a vibrant inner life, especially when the "necessity" for the work is subjective rather than objective: "I do this because I need to be doing something" rather than "I do this because it needs to be done." Work can expand to fill the time available. Just as a partner in a deteriorating relationship can sidestep revealing confrontations by multiplying the hours spent apart from the domestic situation, we often postpone important questions about the quality of our life by working

hard at tasks that will make it impossible for us to reflect on deeper issues. By keeping busy, we absolve ourselves from the need to do some hard thinking. A special form of over-working that is much favored in our times is multitasking. By doing several jobs simultaneously, we ensure that we are somewhat detached from them all. We do none of them particularly well, but we excuse ourselves by referring to the many activities with which we had to be occupied. In contrast, according to the saying of Saint Gregory the Great that has been passed on through the centuries, the wise person concentrates on the one thing necessary: *Age quod agis*, "Do what you are doing."[10] There is a time for everything; do now what has to be done now; for other things there will be another time.

Speed.

Many of our contemporaries seem to be obsessed with speed. The only meaning they find in their work is to finish it so that they can leave it aside. Microscopic savings of time are treasured, even though there is nothing meaningful available to fill the time saved. Speed not only makes us less aware of what is happening around us, it also increases the stress involved in navigating our path through the task. A preoccupation with quantitative progress often diminishes the zeal for a higher quality. As a result, work becomes more burdensome and so increases the tendency to seek recuperation through blanking out by alcohol, television, social media, or some other form of mindless activity. In this case, instead of being wholesome in itself, an activity which is experienced as unsatisfying needs to be counterbalanced by what amounts to actively doing nothing.

---

10. *Homilies on the Gospel* 37.9; *Corpus Christianorum: Series Latina* 141, 355; *Dialogues* 4, 58.1; *Sources Chrétiennes* 265, 194.

Addictions, Compulsions, Habits, and Routines.
All these conditions have the effect of opening up a direct route to an activity—or to inactivity—that does not pass by way of reasonable choice. We obey our inclinations without being fully aware of why we are acting thus, and without submitting the consequences to assessment. Our choices are not based on external evidence, but solely on our interior conditioning. We act like Pavlov's dogs; the response to the stimulus is predictable, immediate, and automatic.

Partiality, Prejudice, Pre-emption.
Often, we see only what we expect to see. Our pre-emptive interpretations distort the evidence so that everything we perceive confirms our anticipations. Fundamentally, this is a survival technique. We distort our perception of the world around us so that it does not challenge our prevailing philosophy of life. Contrary evidence is censored. Often we buttress our willful misperceptions by changing the labels we use: "I am not overweight; I am full-bodied." Those on our side are termed "patriots"; others are "terrorists." We christen self-indulgence as "self-care" and close our eyes to the fact that it is ultimately self-destructive. By refusing to see the world as it is, we guarantee that our responses to reality will always be off-target, any resultant activity will not yield significant results, and so it will be experienced as meaningless. We are averse to real change and one of the ways we avoid its necessity is by changing the labels we affix to things, so that the necessity for any modification is muted.

Grievances from the Past.
We all carry the scars of our past. Sometimes past experiences have been so traumatic that our lives have been seriously blighted. In such a situation we would need specialized care to attain even a basic level of equilibrium. For most of us, how-

ever, these historic wounds are not so serious, but they lurk beneath the surface of consciousness and influence the way that we interact with the world. If, as a child, I was terrorized by a neighbor's dog, I may harbor a lifelong aversion to the canine species. If I was reprimanded by a second-grade teacher and called "stupid," I may well go through life underestimating my intelligence and capabilities. Whether we are prepared to admit it or not, the past continues to influence our choices, interposing itself between us and the world. On a more conscious level, I may bear a resentment at the wrongs that have been done to me by others and spend my life punishing those whom I perceive as the surrogates of my ancient persecutors, whether I do this by positive nastiness or through some form of passive aggression. In such cases, it is clear that I am not interacting with the present but continuing to fight past wars, long after the dust of battle has settled.

Anxieties about the Future.
Fear drives many of the options that we take, although it is often disguised as some other more acceptable emotion: we are fearful because of past experiences; we are fearful because we lack the ability to gauge the possibilities that confront us; we are fearful because we underestimate our own abilities; we are fearful because of our timidity in the face of pressure from others. Fear rushes us into imprudent actions as often as it holds us back from what is appropriate. Fear sets thresholds we dare not cross and ultimately frustrates the realization of our inherent potential. We do not want to pay too much attention to the present moment, lest it should reveal certain courses of action that we know we do not have the courage to take. In some mysterious way, the uncertainty of the future reaches back to cripple the present. We are more concerned with what might happen than what is actually happening now. Fear of the future offsets the impact of the present so that

our ability to gauge an appropriate response is severely restricted. In a similar way, allowing ourselves to become preoccupied with mad schemes that will never be realized means that we will be so concerned with future projects that there will be no energy left to deal with the present.

Many of these inhibiting factors are due to the activation of the "default mode network" in the brain. The default mode network is the coalition of brain regions that integrates and governs such functions as constructing a self-referencing narrative, moral and social reasoning, and remembering the past and imagining the future. Its impact is strongest when we are not consciously and energetically interacting with the world in a focused way. This is the function of the brain that is responsible for selecting and assembling the elements of a personal identity and constructing the autobiographical story that we use as a point of reference in the choices we make. It may be loosely identified with the "Ego." In the absence of conscious engagement with goal-oriented tasks, the default mode network steps in to take over the running of our lives in accordance with the procedure that has been built up over the years. When the default mode network is in charge, there is no free determination of the future, but a reliance on an indefinite continuation of the status quo. We do not respond to present particularities, but squeeze them into familiar patterns that reproduce what has already happened. As a result, our response to reality is always misgauged. When we are not living mindfully, we drift into self-replicating irresponsibility.

A recent study has suggested that consciousness is the result of the discomfort we feel when reality does not correspond with our expectations.[11] If we are driving routinely along a familiar route and suddenly we are diverted to a com-

---

11. See Mark Solms, *The Hidden Spring: A Journey to the Source of Consciousness* (London: Profile Books, 2021).

plicated detour, we immediately become more alert, and perhaps alarmed. Instead of cruising thoughtlessly on our usual trajectory, we have to sit up and pay attention. Similarly, when a life lived smoothly according to the dictates of the default mode network is interrupted, a higher level of attention is demanded of us. This is an expression of the grace of discontinuity. Interruptions can become creative moments. The discomfort occasioned by the unexpected precipitates greater alertness. Mindfulness is not the descent into some somnolescent nirvana, but the sharper awareness of hitherto unnoticed aspects of reality. It is a never-ending process, because a single glance or even a continuing gaze cannot capture the whole reality by which we are confronted.

Living mindfully is an ongoing occupation, though it admits of degrees. It is not the same as taking time out to "do" a "mindfulness meditation." It is a progressive preference for the present moment as the prime carrier of meaning. This is sometimes termed "the sacrament of the present moment." By taking the present seriously, we become more attuned to its particular qualities. Thus we will begin to see opportunities that will yield beneficial results and so, ultimately, will help us live happier and more productive lives.

Adventure

The full truth about the present moment is that it is not complete in itself. It is the overlap of past and future. The way that we process the data of the present is largely conditioned by what we have learned in the past. The ability to learn is an integral part of all living things—certainly of all animals. By experiencing both the positive and negative results of particular actions, we learn what to embrace and what to reject. Cattle learn to avoid electric fences because they remember that touching them is unpleasant; cats learn to present themselves when a spoon is rapped on their feeding dish, because they enjoy eating. We too are conditioned by our experiences of reward and punishment. The way that we assess the quality of each moment depends largely on what we have already experienced. A novice surfer may well be intimidated by the waves known as reef breaks, but to those more experienced, the greater degree of difficulty adds to their exhilaration. What has happened in the past increases the intensity of the impact that the present makes. Human experience is cumulative. Concentrating fully on the present includes bringing the past into purview. Above all, it means not being passive before the onrush of time. Living life to the full involves filling each moment, not leaving time empty, as Dietrich Bonhoeffer noted:

> Time is the most precious gift in our possession, for it is the most irrevocable. This is what makes it so disturbing to look back upon time we have lost. Time lost is time when we have not lived a full human life, time enriched by experience, creative endeavour, enjoyment and suffering. Time lost is time we have not filled, time left empty.[12]

To the extent that we appreciate the role that the past has on the present, we begin to understand that the present also influences the future. This means that I have a responsibility for the outcome of the choices that I make. It may be fun to jump off a cliff, but eventually I will learn that after the freedom of flight through the air I land *splat!* on the ground. Every action has its consequences. In real life, however, the options we face are a little more complicated. More often than not, we

---

12. Dietrich Bonhoeffer, *Letters and Papers from Prison* (London: Collins, 1953), 134.

have to attempt to arrive at a compromise between a range of positive and negative expectations. Buying a red Ferrari may be the dream of a lifetime, but it will severely deplete my savings, it may cause others to dismiss me as frivolous, and it may prompt the traffic police to take an undue interest in me. Perhaps I should stay with my beige Toyota! Part of being human is learning to weave our way around conflicting options and make a responsible choice that will not necessarily be a total and unqualified benefit.

There is always a danger that we are so intimidated by the prospect of collateral damage that we are reluctant to arrive at a decisive choice. It always seems so much safer to do nothing, to sit on our hands in the hope that the situation will resolve itself without our having to do anything. I once saw a humerous postcard with a solitary man sitting on a park bench and bearing the words, "I think I will just sit here until life gets easier." This option is hopeless. "He that observeth the wind, shall not sow, and he that regardeth the clouds, shall not reap" (Eccl 11:4). Taking excessive time to consider all possible options may simply mean that the opportunity expires and further action becomes impossible. The world in which we live is a world of multiple choices; it is statistically unlikely that anyone will always make the right choice. This means that all of us have to live with misjudgments and mistakes and, curiously, it is often through our mistakes that we learn most efficiently. Risk and uncertainty are integral elements of human existence. "For who shall bring him to see what shall be after him?" (Eccl 3:22). "Man knoweth not what shall be: and who can tell him what shall be after him?" (Eccl 10:14). To be paralyzed in the face of multiple possibilities leads us to demand a level of certainty that is superhuman and, therefore, unattainable.

For who knoweth what is good for man in the life
and in the number of the days of the life of his vanity,

seeing he maketh them as a shadow? For who can show unto man what shall be after him under the sun? (Eccl 7:1–2)

Uncertainty is counterbalanced by prudence, which weighs benefits against harms, and knowns against unknowns, and so arrives at a plausibly positive course of action. Often, the rightness of a solution is not absolute, but is determined by the context in which it occurs. Sometimes the right course is counterintuitive. "God also hath made this contrary to that" (Eccl 7:14). What may seem negative to us is ultimately God's doing, and demands appropriate discernment and respect. This is where the wise person has the advantage over the fool. Those who are wise read the moment, and this forms part of the equation by which they arrive at a solution. The timing is important:

I thought in mine heart, God will judge the just and the wicked: for time is there for every purpose and for every work. (Eccl 3:17)

The heart of the wise shall know the time and judgment. For to every purpose there is a time and judgment, because the misery of man is great upon him. For he knoweth not that which shall be: for who can tell him when it shall be? (Eccl 8:7–8)

The opening of Qoheleth's third chapter is well-known and much admired. "To all things there is an appointed time, and a time to every purpose under the heaven" (Eccl 3:1). What often passes unnoticed is that the passage of time implies a constant and ongoing obligation of discernment. Possibilities are not simply good or bad; their moral quality depends on the concordance with the demands of the moment:

To all things there is an appointed time,
and a time to every purpose under the heaven.
A time to be born, and a time to die:
a time to plant, and a time to pluck up that which
      is planted.
A time to slay, and a time to heal:
a time to break down, and a time to build.
A time to weep, and a time to laugh:
a time to mourn, and a time to dance.
A time to cast away stones, and a time to gather
      stones:
a time to embrace, and a time to be far from em-
      bracing.
A time to seek, and a time to lose:
a time to keep, and a time to cast away.
A time to rend, and a time to sew:
a time to keep silence, and a time to speak.
A time to love, and a time to hate:
a time of war, and a time of peace. (Eccl 3:1–8)

This ethical system is very nuanced, in that actions are to be assessed not only according to their intrinsic quality but also according to their appropriateness at a particular moment. The agricultural image is the clearest. Not every season is suitable for sowing seed. Seeds meant to be sown in early spring will never do well if sown midsummer. Not because there is something wrong with the seeds, but simply because it was the wrong time for sowing. Similarly, our whole life is not meant to be spent weeping and mourning; there will be times for laughing and dancing. Alternation is stamped on every aspect of human experience. "Let us avoid being stupid so that our prosperity does not kill us, but in the day of good things, let us not be forgetful of bad things—and vice versa. This present age is a mixture of both, not only for the worldly, but also for the spiritual."[13] "Every human life revolves around these two things: I refer to prosperity and adversity."[14]

Unlike the natural cycles, the seasons of life usually cannot be known in advance. They often come upon us when we are unprepared: "For neither doth man know his time, but as the fishes which are taken in an evil net, and as the birds that are caught in the snare: so are the children of men snared in the evil time when it falleth upon them suddenly" (Eccl 9:12). In other words, we need to develop the skills of reading each moment, discerning the signs of the times. Our experience of the past can help us in this task, but we should be careful not to forget that every moment is unique. The default mode network of our brain encourages us to operate on the basis of business as usual; this may often be practical, but it is by no means infallible, nor does it always yield optimal results. The apparent circularity of temporal existence (cf. Eccl 1:5–7) should not lull us into non-responsiveness. We need to take seriously the particularities of the present, and to leave room in our assessment for the unexpected.

Uncertainty is not necessarily a sufficient justification for inaction. Because we can never know everything, there is scope for risk-taking and boldness: "Cast thy bread upon the waters: for after many days thou shalt find it" (Eccl 11:1). To live mindful of present opportunities implies a willingness to pursue them, even without the comfort of total certainty. Prudence may, however, suggest that we hedge our bets, that we do not put all our eggs in one basket. This implies a willingness to do more rather than less, to diversify. To do many

---

13. Saint Bernard of Clairvaux, *Sermon for Palm Sunday* 2.1; *Sancti Bernardi Opera* 5:46.

14. Saint Bernard of Clairvaux, *Sermon for Palm Sunday* 3.2; *Sancti Bernardi Opera* 5:52.

things in the hope that some of what we do will be profitable: "In the morning sow thy seed, and in the evening let not thine hand rest: for thou knowest not whither shall prosper, this or that, or whether both shall be a like good" (Eccl 11:6).

It is precisely the impermanence of everything under the sun that summons us to respond promptly to each moment as it passes, accepting that our knowledge is limited, that our choices are often contingent on factors beyond our control, and that our capacity to carry projects through to a successful conclusion is uncertain. Qoheleth seems to believe that it is better to do something than to slide into a routine of holding back and waiting for the propitious moment that will never come. Mistakes are inevitable, but relatively few of them are irreversible.

Loving This Life

Solomon, the putative author of the early part of Ecclesiastes, had everything that the human heart desires. Yet having everything left him disillusioned. This points to the conclusion that human happiness is not to be found in the tangible accumulation of what are traditionally thought to be benefits. Riches, pleasures, success, and even wisdom cannot satisfy the human heart. All is vanity. The conclusion must be that if happiness is possible, it is to be sought elsewhere. What Qoheleth is offering us is a question, not an answer. He is posing the puzzle stated by the Psalmist, "Many say 'What can bring us what is good?'" (Ps 4:7). What Qoheleth knows with certainty is that we are surrounded by a world of desired possibilities which do *not* lead to happiness. For the state of bliss that we desire, something else is needed, but what it is he does not say. We have to work it out for ourselves:

Then I thought in mine heart, It befalleth unto me, as it befalleth to the fool. Why therefore do I then labour to be more wise? And I said in mine heart, that this also is vanity. For there shall be no remembrance of the wise, nor of the fool for ever: for that that now is, in the days to come shall all be forgotten. And how dieth the wise man, as doth the fool? Therefore I hated life: for the work that is wrought under the sun is grievous unto me: for all is vanity, and vexation of the spirit. I hated also all my labour, wherein I had travailed under the sun, which I shall leave to the man that shall be after me. And who knoweth whether he shall be wise or foolish? Yet shall he have rule over all my labour, wherein I have travailed, and wherein I have showed myself wise under the sun. This is also vanity. Therefore I went about to make mine heart abhor all the labour wherein I had travailed under the sun. (Eccl 2:15–20)

Qoheleth's response to the complaint he inserted in Solomon's mouth is to assert that, despite the pervading presence of vanity, happiness can be found within the mixity of life. He is under no delusion that life, as we experience it, is always useful, pleasurable, or meaningful. He believes, however, that the fact of consistent change makes life not only tolerable but interesting, enjoyable, and lovable. The chiaroscuro character of life is what calls us to be intellectually alert and, as we mature, to appreciate the specific beauty of both light and darkness. Hunger adds tang to the plainest meal. One who is tired is grateful to sleep anywhere. Absence makes the heart grow fonder.

Here is the delightful paradox of human living. Nothing is permanent. If it is pleasant, enjoy it while it lasts. If it is burdensome, be happy that it will not last forever. Changeableness is not the enemy of joy but can be its ally. Each new circumstance has the capacity to cultivate in us new skills and capabilities that will eventually have the result of enriching our lives. It could almost be said that nothing that does not kill us can harm us. Of course, this presupposes a certain power of resilience that refuses to be permanently cast down by troubles and failures and a realistic willingness to reverse course when the situation demands it.

An important component of this positive approach to life's vicissitudes is the belief that in all that happens around us God the Creator is somehow active: "[God] hath made everything beautiful in [its] time" (Eccl 3:11) and the hand of God is master of all that takes place in our world (Eccl 2:24). Qoheleth's vision of God is fundamentally benign. The portion assigned to human beings is not designed to make them miserable. The expectation is that our life's experience will teach us how to persevere through life's inevitable miseries so that we may come to a deeper and more stable happiness and fulfillment. What God has created is good; our enjoyment of these benefits is not only permissible but an imperative of our nature. There is something perverse in a person who does not enjoy food when hungry or sleep when tired. To the simple and upright, what God has created good is experienced with pleasure.

We may, perhaps, reflect further that in our natural pleasure we will, as we become wiser, begin to experience beyond the pleasure itself a certain delight in recognizing the benevolence of the God who provides it. Just as a good meal is enhanced by knowing that it has been prepared with an abundance of love, and that it is intended as the expression of that love, so our enjoyment of created benefits calls us to look beyond present pleasure to the love which is its origin. This is not to diminish the joy brought by a good meal or a sound sleep but to use these present moments of happiness as a means by which we can lift our hearts in gratitude to the spiritual world from which they derive. This is a point made by Saint Leo the Great (400–461):

> Use visible creatures as they should be used. Just as you use the earth, the sea, the sky, the air, the springs and the rivers. Whatever among them is beautiful and inspires wonder let it be for the praise and glory of their Maker. Do not be dedicated to that light which is the source of joy to birds and snakes, wild beasts and cattle, flies and worms. Reach out to the bodily light with your bodily senses but with all the feeling of your mind embrace that true light that illuminates all who come into the world.[15]

Immediate benefits are, as it were, the foretaste of benefits that derive from beyond this present sphere of existence. Qoheleth does not attempt to describe this transcendent reality; he is content to demonstrate the limitation and contingency of all that constitutes the world of human experience. It has no substance; its dominant character is *hevel*. But, in some way, the present imperfect life is both the symbol and the carrier of something greater than itself. We cannot make contact with the mysterious reality except through what is close at hand. The heavens proclaim the glory of God, but so also do earthly creatures, each according to its own nature. What is real is also revelatory.

The present moment is our doorway to ultimate reality — whatever that is. Qoheleth does not name it, but each one of us, according to our own tribe and culture, will have a mental picture of a reality that is beyond words and concepts. Not an

---

15. St. Leo the Great, *In Nativitate Domini Sermo VII*, 6; *Sources Chrétiennes* 22, 146.

abstraction or a creation of the mind but something mysteriously pre-existing and independent of our mental processes —out there; the Great Unknown. To grow in wisdom, there needs to be a progressive embrace of a realistic humility in the face of this infinite Other—yet this is a humility that is not oppressive or degrading, but one that is full of wonder and exhilaration so that it cries out: "Lord God, how great you are!"

Science is constantly expanding the boundaries of our knowledge. Not only are we finding out about the existence of galaxies beyond galaxies in a seemingly infinite array, but things closer to earth that we have taken for granted for millennia are now shown to be much more complex than we ever guessed. For example, there is much that we do not know about the consciousness of animals. Magpies have a facial recognition capability, octopuses are seen to be intelligent even without any sort of spinal cord, and banded shrimps are said to exhibit both memory and curiosity.[16] Even trees communicate and have empathy.[17] We are very foolish if we assume that we have a comprehensive knowledge of our expanding universe. "As thou knowest not which is the way of the [wind], nor how the bones do grow in the womb of her that is with child: so thou knowest not the work of God that worketh all"

---

16. See, for example, Peter Godfrey-Smith, *Other Minds: The Octopus, the Sea, and the Deep Origins of Consciousness* (New York: Farrar, Straus and Giroux, 2016); *Metazoa: Animal Life and the Birth of Mind* (New York: Farrar, Straus and Giroux, 2020). See also Peter Wohlleben, *The Inner Life of Animals: Surprising Observations from a Hidden World* (London: Vintage, 2017). On the complex subterranean universe and its inhabitants, see Matthew Evans, *Soil: The Incredible Story of What Keeps the Earth and Us Healthy* (Crows Nest, NSW: Murdoch Books, 2021).

17. See Peter Wohlleben, *The Hidden Life of Trees: What They Feel, How They Communicate: Discoveries from a Secret World* (Carlton, Australia: Black Inc., 2016).

(Eccl 11:5). The joy-filled admission of our existential ignorance is a necessary first step in the journey toward wisdom. It opens the heart to wonder and admiration. Even Charles Darwin was moved to admiration by what he had uncovered.[18] We are reminded of the words of the Psalmist:

> When I look at your heavens, the work of your
> fingers,
>   the moon and the stars that you have established;
> [I ask] what are human beings that you are mindful
> of them,
>   mortals that you care for them? (Ps 8:3–4)

The present moment is our point of entry into the totality of existence. It is superior to all other moments because it exists; it is not a memory or an expectation; it simply is. Because the present exists, there is a possibility for us to interact with it. The past has passed and the future has not yet arrived; only the present is susceptible to our input. We do ourselves a great wrong by abandoning the present in the useless hope of being elsewhere. Whether we have just won the lottery or have been sentenced to life in prison, this moment is all we have. Its circumstances are the ingredients from which we can confect our life-defining response. We are who and what we are because of

---

18. See the last sentence of *The Origin of Species*. "There is grandeur in this view of life, with its several powers, having been originally breathed by the Creator into a few forms or into one: and that, whilst this planet has gone cycling on according to the fixed law of gravity, from so simple a beginning endless forms most beautiful and most wonderful have been, and are being evolved." In *Great Books of the Western World* 49 (Chicago: Encyclopedia Britannica, 1993), 243. This sentence was included in the second and later editions of *The Origin of Species* at the behest of Reverend Charles Kingsley, the author of *The Water Babies*, to whom Darwin had sent a copy of his book.

how we deal with the details that confront us in the evolving here and now.

If, like Qoheleth, our view of reality includes God as Creator and Sustainer, then we are obliged to conclude that this moment is of God's making. Whether we approve of it or not is immaterial, since we cannot comprehend the ultimate significance of any fragment of the universe. Our faith in God must lead us to a recognition that God's benign providence is at work in our lives and that the present is the only place of encounter with God. Wishing that things were different and pining away with regret and disappointment because of broken dreams will lead us away from reality and from God. The way of return is to concentrate on the present.

Regarding this present moment, it may be said that good and bad are equally good. To state the paradox at greater length: What we judge to be "good" and what we judge to be "bad" are equally expressive of ultimate goodness. The difference is not in the quality of things but in our subjective assessment of them, whereby we paint them in colors of our own devising. According to the Book of Genesis, all created reality is not only "good" but "very good," because all things alike are sustained within the benign providence of God. Our assessment of things has no bearing on their inherent quality.

That is why we must love this earthly life in all its mixity and even in its apparent failure to conform to what we might consider to be best practice. The present is all we have and, within its borders, it is a vortex of infinite possibilities. This is why there might be some wisdom in greeting the dawn of each new day with the words of the Psalm: "This is the day the LORD has made; let us rejoice and be glad in it" (Ps 118:24). And considering its specificities, whether they seem to bring us happiness or grief, our faith-filled response to everything will be simply "Amen!" "Amen!" "Amen!"